THE WORCESTERSHIRE CRICKET QUIZ BOOK

THE WORCESTERSHIRE CRICKET

QUIZ BOOK

LES HATTON

MAINSTREAM
PUBLISHING

First published in Great Britain in 1989 by
MAINSTREAM PUBLISHING COMPANY (EDINBURGH) LTD
7 Albany Street, Edinburgh EH1 3UG

ISBN 1 85158 285 1 (paper)

British Cataloguing in Publication Data
    Hatton, Les
    The Worcestshire cricket quiz book.
    1. Hereford and Worcester. Worcestershire county
    cricket clubs. Worcestershire county cricket club to
    1989
    I. Title
    796.35'863'094244

ISBN 1-85158-285-1

Typeset in 11 on 13pt Imprint by Bookworm Typesetting, Edinburgh
Printed in Great Britain by Billings & Sons, Worcester

Foreword

It is with considerable pleasure – and a little trepidation too – that I welcome, and introduce to you, Les Hatton's Worcestershire Cricket Quiz Book.

The pleasure comes from knowing the enjoyment that this book assuredly will give to so many Worcestershire followers and to many other sporting folk also. It comes too from knowing the enjoyment and fulfilment Les will have gained in preparing this test of our Worcestershire and cricketing knowledge.

My trepidation is twofold. Firstly, at the time of writing this foreword I haven't tackled (or even seen) any of the questions yet – and in the back of my mind there lingers the thought that the County's Secretary ought to know most (not all!) of the answers. Les's keen research will have taken him into the more obscure corners of our history and achievements – that's where the statisticians and historians get their fun – so I'm certain we are all going to be well tested. The second reason for slight anxiety is that there are certain to be those readers who will be determined *not* to look at the answer pages and who want to seek out the answers for themselves (and there will be the odd one or two who don't like Les's official answers!); there will also be some who find themselves stimulated by the questions in this book to enter heated and argumentative debate. So – when my phone next rings I shall have to try and assess whether the information being sought is to help educate one of our followers, or if it is required to settle a heated dispute or some large financial wager. At such times it is perhaps politic not to know the answer – and at least I can now refer the caller back to the Worcestershire Cricket Quiz Book.

If you find you know the answers to most of the questions put to you here – well done! If you know the answers to very few of the questions asked here, then you are the reader who will have gained most from this book. Congratulations to you too!

Mike Vockins

Introduction

I have tried to arrange this quiz book on Worcestershire cricket so that hopefully it will read like a mini history of a club that has come from rags to comparative riches. The County, at the moment, seems to have the almost perfect blend of youth and experience to perform at the highest level in all types of cricket.

In April, 1989 they will play in Brisbane, Australia against Queensland, which will give them the unique situation of having played first-class cricket on four continents, following their visit to Jamaica in 1965 and Rhodesia in 1966.

Because of the enormous success throughout the club, I make no apologies for using 100 of the questions on the 1988 season. Beaten in two major finals, winners of the Refuge Assurance League again and the cream on the top, of course, the winning of the Britannic Assurance County Championship, meant that Worcestershire had their best ever season.

I would like to take this opportunity of thanking many friends for their help in the production of this book. To Les Jacques for the cover photograph of the 1988 R.A.L. winners, Philip Barker, Don Cairney, John Featherstone, Jack Godfrey, Ian Osborne, Jill Smith, Pauline Boyce, Chris Oldnall and *Berrows Journal* for the help with the photographs, Mike Vockins for his foreword and advice, and last, but certainly not least, my wife Dorothy and daughter Rachel for their hours of diligent typing.

Les Hatton
Wolverhampton
November, 1988

Questions

1 What is the accepted date of the formation of the County Cricket Club?

2 What season did Worcestershire enter the County Championship?

3 Who was Secretary of the club at the time?

4 Who was captain during this first season?

5 Worcestershire opened their season with the first-ever first-class fixture at New Road, but who were the visitors?

6 Who kept wicket for the County on this occasion?

7 Who took 10 wickets for Worcestershire in this match?

8 Who scored most runs in this first season for Worcestershire?

9 Groundsman Fred Hunt joined the Club from which southern County?

10 Who were County Champions for this historic Worcestershire season?

THE EARLY DAYS - 2

11 Who was the first batsman to aggregate 1,000 runs in a season for Worcestershire?

12 Who was the first bowler to take 100 wickets for Worcestershire in a season?

13 Who achieved Worcestershire's first seasonal double of 1,000 runs/100 wickets?

14 Who was Worcestershire's first overseas player?

15 Who was the first Worcestershire professional to appear for the Players v. Gentlemen?

16 Against which County did the brothers W.L. and R.E. Foster score hundreds in each innings of a match in 1899?

17 In matches against Warwickshire in 1899 and 1901 wicket-keeper Tom Straw made unusual headlines. But why?

18 Who partnered H.K. Foster v. Derbyshire in Worcestershire's first ever double century partnership?

19 Which season before the 1914-18 Great War did Worcester-shire finish joint runners-up to Nottinghamshire?

20 Who were the County's first overseas touring side at New Road?

THE FOSTERS – I

21 to 27 The seven Fosters did much for early Worcestershire cricket. Give their full Christian names in order of seniority.

28 What is unique about the cricket/soccer ability of R.E.?

29 Which brother had a son play for the County?

30 Which Worcestershire player was a son of one of the brothers' sisters?

THE FOSTERS – 2

31 What was the profession of their father?

32 Which brother joined Kent after the First World War?

33 Which brother was a Test selector?

34 Which brother became a West End actor?

35 Which brother was initially instrumental in Syd Buller joining the County?

36 For which university did three brothers get their cricket blues?

37 For which other County did Basil appear?

38 At which other sport did all the brothers also excel?

39 Which brother became a regular soldier?

40 Which brother died at Lichfield, Staffs., in 1940?

NICKNAMES

To whom do these nicknames belong?

41 'Sandy'

42 'J.C.'

43 'Tip'

44 'Humpty'
45 'Doc'
46 'Plod'
47 'Bunny'
48 'Percy'
49 'Louie'
50 'Schnozz'

A WORCESTERSHIRE A-Z

(With apologies to X and Z)

51 **A** A Worcestershire knight who scored a first-class double century in India.

52 **B** Yorkshire-born all-rounder who just missed a blue for Cambridge in the 70s.

53 **C** Played one season for Worcestershire and was awarded the D.S.O. and M.C. for gallantry during the Second World War.

54 **D** An Oxford blue who played Club cricket for Bewdley.

55 **E** The first batsman to score a century against Worcestershire having already scored one for them.

56 **F** Died on a Birmingham bus on his way home from work.

57 **G** Played only once for Worcestershire but broadcast on BBC radio on numerous occasions.

58 **H** His brother also played for Worcestershire, but moved to a southern County, returning to the fold after an umpiring spell.

59 **I** A darling of a bowler.

60 **J** Born in the Bahamas, but educated at Malvern.

61 **K** An Australian Oxford blue who scored 602 runs for Worcestershire in 1937.

62 **L** Jamaican fast bowler with Kidderminster connections.

63 **M** Indian-born opener who also played for Essex.

64 **N** Chosen as 12th man for England v. New Zealand at Lord's in 1931.

65 **O** Left-arm fast bowler who spanned the war years.

66 **P** Appeared in one Test Match after leaving Worcester-shire.

67 **Q** Died four days after his 85th birthday.

68 **R** Evesham-born father and son with identical Christian names.

69 **S** West Bromwich-born opener whose son played for the Second XI in the 1980s.

70 **T** Played two matches for Worcestershire, one in 1903 and the next in 1926.

71 **U** One Christian name of this New Zealand-born Cambridge blue.

72 **V** Only one match for Worcestershire but successful in South Africa.

73 **W** A wicket-keeper with a Worcester Royal Grammar School and Oxford University background.

74 **Y** Keen on the form book, but that's not so unusual at Worcester!

PICTURE QUIZ – I

75 Name the church on the left of the skyline.

76 St Andrews on the right is better known as?

77 No prizes for guessing 'Roly' Jenkins, but who are the two Test players with him, neither of whom played for Worcestershire?

78 Who played against Worcestershire here in the County Championship?

79 Another Championship match was arranged for the following season but was later moved to New Road. Who were the opposition?

80 Dudley, now unfortunately devoid of cricket, played host to which touring side in 1912?

81 Name the five persons in this 1968 photograph.

82 Name the players sampling Guinness etc., whilst visiting the largest brewery in the world.

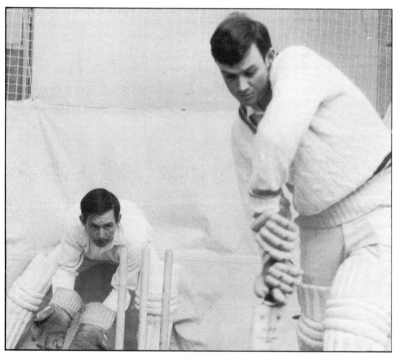

83 Who is the batsman in the indoor nets at Edgbaston?
84 And the wicket-keeper?

85 18 August, 1984 with former players reassembled to celebrate the 20th anniversary of Worcestershire's first winning of the County Championship. However, three persons on this photograph did not appear in the County Championship side that season. Who are they?

FAMILY LINKS - I

86 Who are the two brothers who shared a century opening partnership for Worcestershire?

87 Basil and Damian D'Oliveira both scored hundreds against Surrey in the Sunday League, and in doing so they each hit a six off which Surrey bowler?

88 Who were the last two brothers to play together for England in a Test Match?

89 Which nephew of 'Roly' Jenkins left Worcestershire to join Somerset?

90 Apart from the Foster brothers, which other two brothers appeared for Worcestershire against Yorkshire in 1899?

91 Name the grandfather and grandson who played cricket for Worcestershire and soccer for Worcester City.
92 Name two Worcestershire brothers (born in Chile) and their nephew, who all played for the County.
93 Name the two Worcestershire brothers who lost their lives in the 1914-18 World War.
94 Name a member of the current staff who has not played in the Second XI Championship for Worcestershire, and name his father, who has.
95 Two brothers played for Worcestershire Seconds, but only one of them graduated to the First XI. The other brother still plays Birmingham League cricket. Name both brothers.

AUTOGRAPHS – I

Can you identify these Worcestershire signatures?

96

97

98

99

100

101

102

103

104

105

Identify these hands.

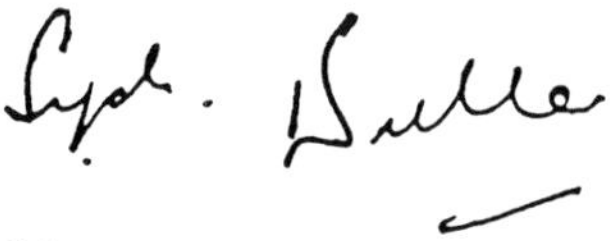

106

107

108

109

19

110

111

112

113

114

115

SURNAMES – I

Identify the following Worcestershire players by their Christian names.

116 Cecil Brabazon
117 Thomas William

118 John Sydney

119 Percy Frederick

120 Ronald Ernest

121 Ivan Nicholas

122 Lawrence Kilner

123 John Alfred

124 Keith Rodney

125 Michael Stephen Anthony

ALL-ROUNDERS

126 Who was the last player to complete the 1,000 runs/100 wickets double in a season for Worcestershire?

127 Dick Howorth did this double in 1939, but who also shared this achievement with him in the same season?

128 Who is the only Worcestershire player to score a hundred and do the hat-trick in the same match?

129 Who is the only Worcestershire player to aggregate 1,000 runs and take 100 wickets in a Sunday League career?

130 Who is the player who missed this double by just eight runs?

131 Who is one of only six players in the history of the Sunday League to score a fifty and take five wickets in the same match?

132 Who was the first overseas-born player to complete a first-class double for Worcestershire?

133 Who is the only player to score 10,000 runs and take 1,000 wickets for Worcestershire?

134 Who scored a double century and took ten wickets in the same match?

135 Who was the last player to score a century and take ten wickets in the same match?

ANAGRAMS

136 NAOMY HUDIES (. . . . .)
137 IVALEN MISCHOCK (. . . . .)
138 DELLINGS TANNOREXEA (. . . . .)
139 WILSON THIKKIEN (. . . . .)
140 DAVIS BELLAIRIO (. . . . .)
141 STEFFORY FOREGE (. . . . .)
142 DUNOAL GRIPPE (. . . .   .)
143 COLONEL DWARDELL (. . . . .)
144 MARTIN HOWNING (. . . . .)
145 MARY HELOUR (. . . . .)

NEW ROAD, WORCESTER – I

These questions concern the ground, its keepers and administrators.

146 For whom did W.G. Grace make his one and only appearance at New Road?
147 Who played the West Indies in a Prudential World Cup Group Match in 1983?
148 Which former Surrey player took over as groundsman on the retirement of Fred Hunt?
149 When was the Supporters' Association formed?
150 At which cathedral was Secretary Mike Vockins ordained on Sunday, 26 June, 1988?
151 Which other Reverend gentleman was Honorary Secretary of the club?
152 Who was the Secretary during the Second World War?
153 Who became Secretary in 1945?
154 When was the present scoreboard first used?
155 Who is the Treasurer of the Supporters' Association?

THE TWENTIES

156 How many times did they finish bottom of the County Championship in this period?

157 During this period what was their best position in this competition?

158 Who captained them on most occasions?

159 Who scored most runs for Worcestershire in the twenties?

160 And who took the most wickets?

161 Who was the wicket-keeper/batsman in 1920 who scored a century on his County Championship debut, the first time this had been achieved for Worcestershire?

162 Which Somerset bowler took all ten Worcestershire wickets at Worcester in 1921?

163 Which two batsmen shared a partnership of 306 for the third wicket against Northants in 1923? A Worcestershire record until 1962.

164 What was later unusual about these two batsmen?

165 Which Nottinghamshire batsman scored a century at New Road on his 50th birthday?

FRED ROOT

166 Which was the county of his birth?

167 When did he make his Worcestershire debut?

168 For which Birmingham League club did he play during his qualifying period?

169 How many Test appearances did he make?

170 Of what type of bowling was he reputed to be the innovator?

171 He is the only bowler to take 200 wickets in a season for Worcestershire, but which season?

172 Who was his captain on his only M.C.C. tour abroad in 1925/26?

173 He has Worcestershire's best innings bowling figures of 9-23, but who was this against?

174 He did the double once for Worcestershire, but in which season?

175 Which Lancashire League club did he join on leaving Worcestershire?

176 Richard Illingworth (pictured) is the third Yorkshire-born slow left-arm bowler to play for Worcestershire. Harry Wilson was the first, from 1901-06, but who was the second?

177 Did any of them play for the County of their birth?

178 Maurice Nichol (pictured) scored a century for Worcestershire on his first-class debut. Who was the last to achieve this
for Worcestershire?

179 Worcestershire played two home matches at this venue, Essex, in 1910, and Surrey in 1911. Where is this majestic pavilion?

180 Name this son of a famous father in the Worcestershire nets.

181 Who is this former Worcestershire player who moved to another County?

182 Name the four players pictured during pre-season training in 1978.

183 For which Australian state side did the player second from the right make his first-class debut in 1977?

184 Fred Bowley (pictured) held the record individual innings score of 276 until beaten by Glenn Turner in 1982. Who were Bowley's opponents?

185 But where and when?

Can you identify the surnames of these players?

186 David Mark
187 Frederick Edward
188 William Herbert
189 Collis Llewellyn
190 Howard Gordon
191 Charles Victor
192 Robert Gillespie
193 Alan Esmond
194 Charles Duncan
195 William Victor

WICKET-KEEPERS

196 Who kept wicket once for Worcestershire and had a son who later played cricket for Kent, soccer for Charlton Athletic and fly-fished for England?

197 Who was the only wicket-keeper to be officially appointed captain of Worcestershire?

198 In 1988 Steve Rhodes had 29 Sunday League dismissals. Whose record of 28 did he beat?

199 Which amateur wicket-keeper died in Dorset in 1984, and was the son of a Warwickshire and England batsman?

200 Which wicket-keeper played 18 times for Worcestershire and later became groundsman at New Road?

201 Which 1920s Worcestershire wicket-keeper in a local club match helped dismiss the first five batsmen from behind the stumps and then went on to bowl and take the last five wickets?

202 Who is the wicket-keeper who played for Notts before the Second World War, and Middlesex and Worcestershire after, but was better-known for his cricket with Sir Julian Cahn's XI?

203 Which former Worcestershire wicket-keeper received the M.B.E. in June 1965?

204 Where did Hugo Yarnold stump six batsmen (four off Jenkins, two off Bradley) in an innings for Worcestershire in 1951?

205 In 1964 Roy Booth helped dismiss 100 batsmen. In which year was his total 101?

206 Who was the last Oxford blue to keep wicket for Worcestershire?

207 Which Worcestershire wicket-keeper deputised for Alan Knott in an England v. The Rest Test Trial?

208 Which Worcestershire wicket-keeper is the only player to have scored a first-class century at Stourport?

209 Which Worcestershire wicket-keeper, scorer of one first-class century, toured Australia and New Zealand in 1922-23 with A.C. Maclaren's M.C.C. side?

210 Worcestershire have had many Yorkshire-born wicket-keepers, but which one of them was understudy to Hugo Yarnold between 1952 and 1953?

FOOTBALLING CRICKETERS

211 Which Worcestershire all-rounder kept goal in the 1963-64 FA Cup final?

212 With which club did George Dews make his Football League debut?

213 Which other Worcestershire cricketer played soccer for the same club?

214 With which club did Ted Hemsley finish his football League career?

215 Which Worcestershire cricketer was a member of an FA Cup/First Division Championship double side?

216 Which Wembley Cup final had Jim Cumbes keeping goal for Aston Villa?

217 Which Wolves footballer had a match bowling analysis of 15-87?

218 Henry Horton played League soccer with three clubs, two of them being Bradford and Southampton. Which was the other club?

219 Which Worcestershire cricketer scored a hat-trick on his English International soccer debut?

220 Which former Birmingham City goalkeeper played second-eleven cricket for Worcestershire between 1964 and 1966?

STOURBRIDGE

221 When did Worcestershire play their first County Championship match here?

222 In this opening match which Worcestershire batsman scored a double century?

223 Which English first-class record was performed at Stourbridge?

224 Which Worcestershire batsman scored 161 in this match only to finish on the losing side by an innings and 33 runs?

225 Bob Broadbent held six catches off Worcestershire bowlers here in the second innings of which visiting county in 1960?

226 Who is the only batsman to score a century in each innings of a match at Stourbridge?

227 This was Worcestershire's last first-class match at Stourbridge starting on the Wednesday that Prince Charles married Lady Diana. Who are the four players who played for Worcestershire still connected with the club?

228 Name two Northants players with Worcestershire connections.

229 In 1936 Worcestershire recorded their first victory over Yorkshire for 27 years. Which visiting Test Match batsman was dismissed for a 'pair'?

230 Only 469 runs for the loss of 40 wickets were scored during this match. However, which Worcestershire batsman hit four sixes and four fours in the highest innings of the match off an attack that included Hedley Verity?

231 Which Stourbridge stalwart, not a member of the Worcestershire staff, made national newspaper headlines for domestic
reasons not unconnected with one's love for cricket?

232 Who were the first visitors to Stourbridge in the John Player
League?

233 Which Derbyshire bowler took 16 wickets for 84 runs here in
1952?

234 The last match played at Stourbridge by Worcestershire was
a Sunday League match in 1982. Who were the visitors?

235 Who captained them?

'DOC' GIBBONS

236 Although known as 'Doc' throughout his career, with what
names was he christened?

237 How was he supposed to have earned this nickname?

238 When did he make his Worcestershire debut?

239 For whom, in the Birmingham League, did he spend his
qualifying period?

240 Apart from three matches, all his first-class career was with
Worcestershire. In 1928 he appeared twice for the Players
against the Gentlemen, but in which other match did he
appear?

241 How many first-class centuries did he score?

242 His highest innings was 212 not out at Dudley. Who was this
against?

243 He carried his bat through a completed innings twice, both
on the same ground, but which ground?

244 In which season did he achieve the record Worcestershire
aggregate of 2,654 runs?

245 In 1939 he scored a hundred in each innings of a match for
the only time in his career. Who was this against?

246 He took just seven wickets during his career of 383 matches,
three of them on his debut. Who were the opposition?

247 What was unusual about his first two centuries?

248 In 1928 against the West Indies he shared in two consecutive
double-century partnerships. 207 for the second wicket with

Maurice Nichol, but who was his partner for the 214 unbroken for the third wicket?

249 After the war he played in just three first-class matches at the age of 41. Where did he play his final innings?

250 What career did he follow on leaving first-class cricket?

BOOKS

251 Which Worcestershire all-rounder, better-known after his playing days, wrote *How's That?*?

252 Who wrote *A Time To Declare*?

253 Which group of cricket followers produced in 1985 *Cricket Grounds of Worcestershire*?

254 Who assisted Imran Khan with his 1983 book *Imran*?

255 Who wrote *A Cricket Pro's Lot*?

256 Which year did Tom Graveney write *On Cricket*?

257 Who, in 1952, wrote a short history of Worcestershire in the *County Cricket Series*?

258 Who wrote two longer histories of Worcestershire?

259 What is the title of Graham Dilley's book published in 1988?

260 Who wrote *Worcestershire County Cricket Club, A Pictorial History*?

NEW ROAD – 2

261 Who was the first Worcestershire cricketer to be Secretary of the club?

262 Only one first-class match not involving Worcestershire has been played at New Road. What was the occasion?

263 Who scored a hundred in each innings during this match?

264 Who was the scorer when Worcestershire won the County Championship in 1964?

265 Which groundsman in the 1970s won the 'Groundsman of the Year' award on three occasions?

266 When did Mike Vockins become Secretary of the club?

267 Scorer Jim Sewter played cricket for which Birmingham League club?

268 The Ladies' Pavilion is famous for its teas, but when did the present building open?

269 What important purchase did the Supporters' Association help to make in 1976?

270 Who is the assistant groundsman to Roy MacLaren?

TO WORCESTERSHIRE FROM . . .

Cricketers who have joined Worcestershire having appeared for other Counties. Name their previous County.

271 J.J. Bowles
272 C.H. Bull
273 G.R. Cass
274 P.B. Fisher
275 J. Fox
276 W.R. Genders
277 F. Harry
278 B.E. Krikken
279 A.F.T. White
280 J.P. Whitehead

FROM WORCESTERSHIRE TO . . .

Cricketers who have left Worcestershire to join other Counties. Where did they go?

281 R. Berry
282 L.G. Crawley
283 L.N. Devereux
284 H. Horton
285 B.P. King
286 J.F. Maclean
287 P.E. Murray-Willis

288 P.E. Richardson
289 M.S. Scott
290 D.M. Young

PICTURE QUIZ – 3

291 Worcestershire 1936. What is the name of the ancestral home of the captain?
292 Who is the future captain of the County inset in the centre?
293 For which County did the player on the extreme left of the back row appear immediately after the Second World War?
294 Who are the two Stourbridge-born players in the photograph?
295 Who are the three non-English players in the photograph?
296 Who is the only Geordie in the picture?

297   Who is this Worcestershire batsman who played four times
        for England at soccer?

298 What was unique about these four Worcestershire players only to be equalled in 1961?

299 Who is this Worcestershire player?

300 George Gaukrodger kept wicket on occasions for Worcestershire from 1900-1910. Where was he born?

301 This photograph was taken at the *Sunday Mail* cricket awards at the end of the 1987 season. Worcestershire players won three of the awards: Graeme Hick (batting), Neal Radford (bowling) and Steve Rhodes (wicket-keeping). Who is the odd man out with the fielding award?

TEST MATCH SPECIALS

All questions relate to Worcestershire cricketers.

302 Who made his Test debut at Sydney in the first Test of the 1932-33 'body line' series?

303 Ted Arnold took a wicket with his first ball in Test cricket but who was his illustrious victim?

304 Which batsman was the first in Test cricket history to score a fifty in each innings of his first England v. Australia Test without reaching a hundred in either of them?

305 Who was the first Worcestershire player to captain England?

306 Which bowler made his Test debut in a match that had only 50 minutes' play owing to heavy rain?

307 Who was the first player to represent England after the Second World War?

308 Who was the first Test player to play for Worcestershire in a first-class match?

309 Which player followed his father into Test cricket?

310 Who made his Test debut in the 'timeless test' in Durban in 1938-39?

311 Which Worcestershire captain took six wickets on his Test debut and finished with eight in the match?

312 Who was the first Worcestershire first-class cricketer to umpire a Test Match?

313 Which bowler played in only two Test Matches but took five wickets in the first innings of each of them?

314 Where did 'Roly' Jenkins make his Test debut?

315 Which former president of the M.C.C. made his Test debut when a Worcestershire cricketer?

316 Which batsman played Test cricket for two countries?

REG PERKS

317 When did Reg make his first-class debut for Worcestershire?

318 He played for England twice, once on tour in South Africa. Who was his captain on this tour?

319 Hammond captained Perks for his other Test Match but who were the opposition?

320 He performed two hat-tricks for Worcestershire, one at Stourbridge in 1931 against Kent. Who was the other against?

321 Who was the batsman, later to be knighted, to become his first first-class wicket?

322 Who was his County captain during his first season in first-class cricket?

323 He is the only bowler to take more than 2,000 wickets for the County. What was his final aggregate?

324 Of these wickets his best was 162 against which County?

325 He failed to take 100 wickets against just three Counties – Lancashire (82), and Yorkshire (85), but who was the third?

326 He was the first professional to be appointed captain of Worcestershire during his last season in first-class cricket. Name the year.

327 Worcestershire finished bottom of the County Championship once in this period. Which season?

328 Which two Gloucestershire players at Worcester in 1933 equalled the 1899 record set by R.E. and W.L. Foster of the same two batsmen scoring centuries in each innings of a match?

329 Tragedy struck the cricket world when Maurice Nichol was found dead in his hotel bed on Whit Monday morning, 1933. Where were Worcestershire playing during this sad weekend?

330 Which Worcestershire player captained England at Trent Bridge in the first Test against the 1934 Australians?

331 Which visiting 18-year-old batsman scored the first of his 129 centuries at New Road in 1934?

332 Which visiting bowler, who went on to be a world-renowned coach, took four wickets in four balls at Worcester in 1935?

333 In 1936 at Stourbridge, Worcestershire had an 11-run victory over a side that they had not beaten since 1909. Who were the visitors?

334 A bowler took ten Worcestershire first-innings wickets at New Road in 1936. Who performed this magic act and returned to sit next to Jim Sewter on many occasions in later years?

335 Which Australian batsman became the second Worcestershire overseas player to appear for the Gentlemen against the Players?

336 Which bowler took 29 Worcestershire wickets in two Championship matches in 1937?

337 Why did the Worcestershire bowlers' hourly rate deteriorate in 1939?

338 Which Worcestershire batsman of this period won the English Open Men's Doubles table tennis title three times between 1928 and 1930 with the legendary Fred Perry as his partner?

339 Which bowler took the last wicket for Worcestershire prior to the Second World War and completed the 1,000 runs/100 wickets double for the season?

340 Who scored most runs for Worcestershire during this period?

341 And who took most wickets?

DUDLEY - I

342 When was the first County Championship match at Tipton Road?

343 Who were the visitors?

344 Who scored the first first-class century there?

345 Which visiting batsman scored 305 not out in 1914?

346 In 1934 Gloucestershire scored 625-6 with three batsmen scoring centuries – W.R. Hammond 265* and C.J. Barnett 170 – but who was the batsman who scored 104?

347 Who has the best bowling figures there?

348 Which Worcestershire batsman scored three centuries at Dudley against Worcestershire?

349 When did Dudley stage their last full week of County Championship cricket with matches against Warwickshire and Surrey?

350 Which Worcestershire bowler was hit for three sixes and a four off consecutive deliveries by George Lambert (Gloucestershire) in 1949?

351 Which New Zealand-born bowler had career-best figures of 8-20 there in 1950?

DUDLEY - 2

352 Which Worcestershire bowler had his Sunday League career best at Dudley in 1975?

353 Who is the only batsman to score a Sunday League century there?

354 In 1975 Glenn Turner scored 30 off the opening over of a John Player League match. Who was the unfortunate bowler?

355 The lowest County Championship score at Dudley is 68 by Worcestershire against Gloucestershire. Which visiting bowler took 10-78 in the match?

356 Who was the last Worcestershire batsman to score a County Championship century there?

357 In 1972 Worcestershire were the first County to record two consecutive Sunday League century partnerships. Glenn Turner and Ron Headley put 125 together for the first wicket, but who helped the former add 120 for the second?

358 Who is the only bowler to take five wickets there in a Sunday League innings?

359 When was the last first-class match at Dudley?

360 Who were the visitors?

361 14 Sunday League games were played at Dudley, but who were the last opposition in 1977?

DICK HOWORTH

362 When did he make his first-class debut for Worcestershire?

363 Which was the county of his birth?

364 For which Birmingham League club did he play during his qualifying period?

365 He scored three centuries for Worcestershire, but only one of them came after the 1939-45 War. Who was this against?

366 In 1947 he took a wicket with his first ball in Test cricket. Who was his South African victim?

367 Who was the captain on his only M.C.C. tour abroad?

368 Where did this tour take place?

369 In 1950 he performed the only hat-trick of his first-class career. Who were the opposition?

370 How many times did he do the 'double'?

371 He took 124 wickets in his last season. Which year was this?

Name these venues.

372 Where Worcestershire played two County Championship matches off the mainland of Great Britain.

373 Younis Ahmed scored a match-winning century here in 1980, when County Championship cricket was first played at this seaside venue.

374 Two Sunday League trips here have been high-scoring affairs with a total of 35 sixes struck in the two matches.

375 Worcestershire won by 64 runs in 1949 on their one-and-only visit to this quiet cathedral city in the south. The opposition included two sets of brothers.

376 Ray East took five wickets for Essex in 1969 during Worcestershire's only visit to this venue.

377 Worcestershire have played one Championship and one Sunday League match at this Yorkshire venue, and this over a four-day period.

378 Basil D'Oliveira took five Sunday League wickets here in 1972.

379 Fred Root took 8-25 here in 1925 on a ground that he must have visited quite often during his days as a Lancashire League professional.

380 A close encounter of the wrong kind took place at Titwood, but thanks to sensible batting by Tim Curtis and Richard Illingworth the County saved their blushes. In which city did this take place?

381 A 'posh' Northants side beat Worcestershire by an innings here in 1933, thanks to V.W.C. Jupp's ten wickets in the match and 113 by A.G. Liddell.

382 Roger Knight captained his side to victory by 227 runs in 1983 during Worcestershire's last visit here despite a century from Dipak Patel.

383 Worcestershire's best match bowling figures were performed here by a former Wolves footballer, many years ago.

384 Frank Watson (no, not of Worcester Cricket Call fame) scored a century here when Lancashire went roving from Old Trafford for this innings victory in 1933.

385 Another cathedral city, visited only once by Worcestershire, but this time in the West Country. Worcestershire won by an innings here in 1935 thanks to 131 from G.E.B. Abell (later Sir George) and match figures of 10-48 from Reg Perks.

386 Worcestershire's first tie in the Sunday League took place at this venue in 1973 and featured two centuries in the same match for the first time in the competition by Basil D'Oliveira and Graham Roope.

387 David Banks, Neal Radford and Steve Rhodes made their Worcestershire Nat-West Trophy debuts here and helped defeat a minor County in the first round.

388 Worcestershire played one Championship match at May's Bounty in 1938 and a Sunday League match forty years later. Name the town.

389 A rare Yorkshire home ground, but Worcestershire managed to lose here twice, before the First World War, quite easily.

390 Worcestershire have played five times at Ynysangharad Park but where would you find this Glamorgan venue?

391 A visit to Shropshire where a Walsall bowler, Derek Nicholls, took six wickets and the Gold Award from adjudicator Geoff Pullar in 1982.

392 Rain interfered with this match, but a helicopter was used to accelerate the drying conditions. Who were the visitors to New Road?

393 This photograph was taken during the visit of the Archbishop of Canterbury to celebrate the 13th centenary anniversary of the Worcestershire diocese on Sunday, 18 May 1980. The ground was cleared in time to entertain which side in the Sunday League on the same afternoon?

394 No longer a Worcestershire player, but where is he now?

395 Graeme Hick began his English cricket career with Kidderminster in the Birmingham League scoring 1,234 runs in the 1984 season (as well as 964 for Worcestershire Second XI). Who is the only Worcestershire cricketer to have scored more runs in a Birmingham League season?

396 A Worcestershire Second XI photograph of 1966. Who is the
     only person in the group ever to play Test cricket?
397 Name the three professional Football League players in the
     photograph.
398 Len Beel never played any first-class cricket but appeared in
     just one John Player League game. Who was this for?

399 Who were Worcestershire's first opponents at Chester Road in 1921?

400 Who captained Worcestershire in this match?

401 With the exception of the war years, the County appeared here once each season after 1921. When did this sequence end?

402 Who scored the first double century at Kidderminster?

403 Only two Counties have never played at Kidderminister. One is Gloucestershire, but who is the other?

404 Who are the most regular visitors?

405 When County Cricket returned there in 1987 who kept wicket for the visitors?

406 Les Jackson (Derbyshire) dismissed R.G. Broadbent, R. Morris and D.B. Pearson to complete a hat-trick in 1958. What was unusual about this performance?

407 Worcestershire have played one John Player Sunday League match here. Who were the visitors?

408 Which year did the above match take place?

409 Which batsman has the highest innings at Kidderminster?

410 Which bowler has the best innings figures there?

411 Worcestershire's only County Championship tie ever took place at Kidderminster in 1939. Who were the visitors?

412 Which future England captain was one of Jack Flavell's hat-trick victims here in 1951?

413 Who helped Tim Curtis add 110 for the seventh wicket here in 1987?

414 When did he make his first-class debut for Worcestershire?

415 Which was his last season?

416 How many Test appearances did he make for England?

417 He scored one first-class century. Who was this against?

418 How many times did he complete the 1,000 runs/100 wickets double in a season?

419 He performed three hat-tricks, all of them against Surrey, including one in each innings of the same match at Worcester. Which year did this take place?

420 Which Surrey Test cricketer was a victim in both of them?

421 He went on one M.C.C. tour abroad. Who was his captain?

422 He took 1,005 County Championship wickets, but against one County he took over 100 wickets. Name the County.

423 On leaving first-class cricket he went into the Birmingham League. For whom did he play?

DON KENYON – I

424 For whom did he score a first-class hundred against Worcestershire?

425 Who captained England when Don made his Test debut?

426 Which Birmingham League club did he play for prior to joining the Worcestershire staff?

427 Which season did he become the regular Worcestershire captain?

428 How many centuries did he score for Worcestershire?

429 At the end of which season did he retire from first-class cricket?

430 Who was his opening partner in his last first-class innings?

431 Where did this take place?

432 How many Test appearances did he make for England?

433 He failed to record a first-class century against just one County. Which County?

THE FORTIES

434 Who scored Worcestershire's first double century after the Second World War?

435 Which batsman on his debut for Worcestershire in 1946 was dismissed first ball by the same Lancashire bowler, Eric Price, in each innings of the match at Old Trafford?

436 Three Worcestershire players appeared for Combined Services at New Road against the County in 1946. Leading Aircraftsman Don Kenyon and Company Sergeant Major Reg Perks were joined by which member of the Senior Service?

437 What was different about the Don Bradman innings at Worcester in 1948?

438 How many double centuries did he score against Worcester-shire?

439 Which other Australian batsman scored a century in the 1948 match?

440 Which Worcestershire bowler dismissed both Bradman and Morris and finished with figures of 6-135?

441 Which season did Worcestershire finish third in the County Championship, their best position since 1907?

442 Two Worcestershire players toured South Africa with the M.C.C. party of 1948-49. One of them, 'Roly' Jenkins, made his Test debut, but who was the other?

443 Which overseas player returned to play one more match for Worcestershire after a gap of 11 years?

444 Hugo Yarnold achieved two Worcestershire wicket-keeping records in 1949. One was of nine dismissals in a match, but what was the other?

445 In 1949, Peter Jackson and Hugo Yarnold added 92 for the last wicket against Warwickshire at New Road. Whose benefit match was it?

446 During this period, who captained Worcestershire most times?

447 Who scored most runs for Worcestershire during this period?

448 And who took most wickets?

THE RICHARDSONS

449 Where were Peter and Dick born?

450 When did they first appear together at first-class level?

451 They have a younger brother Bryan who played 40 first-class matches but not for Worcestershire. For whom did he make these appearances?

452 They played against each other in unusual circumstances in two matches at Scarborough and one at Lord's in the late fifties. What were the occasions?

453 Peter moved to Kent in 1959, but for which of the two Counties did he make the most appearances?

454 When did Dick have his benefit at Worcestershire?

455 For which Birmingham League club did they both play before becoming Worcestershire regulars?

456 In 1961 Dick held a record number of catches in a season for Worcestershire. How many were there?

457 When did Peter take over the captaincy of Worcestershire?

458 What has Peter got in common with Bill Edrich, Wally Hammond and Jack Parsons?

LEN COLDWELL

459 For which County did he play in the Minor Counties Championship?

460 When did he make his Worcestershire debut?

461 How many wickets did he take for Worcestershire?

462 He did the hat-trick twice, once against Leicestershire at Stourbridge in 1957, but which current batsman was his first victim in the other?

463 His best bowling performance was 8-38 at Worcester in 1965. Who was this against?

464 How many Test appearances did he make?

465 He toured Australia and New Zealand in 1962/63, but who captained the M.C.C. party?

466 Against which touring side did he have the bowling figures of 7-53?

467 What was the year of his benefit?

468 Though not renowned for his batting, he hit sixes off three consecutive balls at The Oval in 1961. Who was the unfortunate bowler?

469 Who took over the Worcestershire captaincy after his retirement?

470 When did he become President of Worcestershire?

471 Of which local cricket society is he also President?

472 He made one overseas M.C.C. tour. Where did this take place?

473 What important position has he shared, at different times, with former County captains H.K. Foster, R.E.S. Wyatt and N. Gifford?

474 How many 'Man of the Match' awards did he win in the Gillette Cup?

475 Against which County did he aggregate most runs in his career?

476 He has scored the highest individual innings against Yorkshire this century. Where did this take place?

477 What was his score?

478 Where was he born?

WINTER EMPLOYMENT

479 Glenn Turner played the majority of his first-class cricket in New Zealand for Otago, but where did he move for the 1976-77 season?

480 In 1987-88 Phil Newport had his career-best score of 86 in the South African Bowl final. For whom was he playing?

481 For which Australian state side did Rodney Cass appear between 1970 and 1973?

482 John Inchmore had one season of first-class cricket in South Africa. For which Currie Cup side did he appear?

483 Ron Headley played two seasons of Shell Shield cricket in the West Indies, but for which side?

484 Graham Dilley's career-best bowling is 7-63, but in which country did this take place?

485 Vanburn Holder made his Worcestershire debut in 1968, but had already played first-class cricket for which side?

486 Which former Worcestershire player umpired the third Test between India and England at Madras in February, 1934?

487 Where did Graeme Hick play his first first-class cricket outside of Zimbabwe?

488 On leaving Worcestershire in 1970 Tom Graveney played first-class cricket in Australia. For which Sheffield Shield side did he appear?

489 Worcestershire 1984, but who is third from the left on the back row?

490 Who had a benefit that year?

491 Who is fourth from the right on the back row and played against Worcestershire last season?

492 Worcestershire v. the 1956 Australians. Who is on the extreme right of the back row?

493 Which County did he join on leaving Worcestershire?

494 Who is the only university blue in the photograph?

495 Centre of the back row, Bob Broadbent (12th man in this match) took six catches in one innings for Worcestershire at Stourbridge. Who were the opposition?

496 'Laddie' Outschoorn – front row, extreme right – played for which Birmingham League club during his qualifying period?

497 Where is this first-class cricket ground in Worcestershire?

498 Who did the County play here in 1951?

499 Who scored the only century in this match?

500 Who is the batsman in this Sunday League match in 1976?
501 And the wicket-keeper?

JACK FLAVELL

502 Where was he born?

503 With which club did he play in the Football League?

504 At which position?

505 When did he make his Test debut?

506 In how many Tests did he play?

507 How many wickets did he take for Worcestershire?

508 Where did he score his only first-class fifty?

509 What were his best bowling figures for Worcestershire?

510 How many hat-tricks did he perform?

511 What was unusual about one of them?

512 With which village club did he play before joining Worcestershire?

513 Which season did he top the national bowling average?

514 When was he one of Wisden's 'Five Cricketers of the Year'?

515 Which was his last season in first-class cricket?

516 What was the name of his successful restaurant?

THE FIFTIES

517 During the 1950 season the death of a Worcestershire stalwart at the age of 76 was announced. Who was this former player?

518 Which Worcestershire player was one of Wisden's 'Five Cricketers of the Year' for 1950?

519 Who helped 'Laddie' Outschoorn add 198 for the fourth wicket against Essex at Romford with an innings of 118 and can still be seen almost daily when there is cricket at New Road?

520 Who made his Worcestershire debut in 1950 having played table tennis for England seven months before?

521 Don Kenyon, George Dews and 'Roly' Jenkins scored 131 runs in 32 minutes to beat Notts by nine wickets with three minutes to spare. Name the Notts captain who sportingly allowed his bowlers to deliver 12.1 overs in this short time?

522 At Taunton in 1951 Worcestershire needed a six off the last ball of the match to win. Who struck the ball from Bertie Buse into the old pavilion to achieve this exciting victory?

523 Which former Worcestershire player hit 123 against them at Dudley in 1952?

524 Worcestershire fielded their youngest ever player in 1953 against Glamorgan at Worcester, a record that still exists. Who was this young man, who, incidentally never played first-class cricket again?

525 Another 16-year-old played his only first-class match in 1955 against Cambridge University at Worcester. Who was this Wolverhampton-born player?

526 Worcestershire were dismissed for 25 and 40 by Surrey at The Oval in 1955. Who was the only batsman to reach double figures in either innings?

527 In 1955 what did Worcestershire uniquely achieve against the touring South Africans?

528 In 1958 Doug Slade took a wicket with his second ball in first-class cricket by having which Somerset Australian batsman caught by Dick Richardson?

529 Umpire Syd Buller called which Worcestershire bowlers for throwing in 1959?

530 Don Kenyon was obviously the leading Worcestershire run-scorer in this decade, but have a guess, to the nearest 1,000, how many?

531 Who took most wickets for Worcestershire in this period?

RON HEADLEY

532 Of which Birmingham League club was his father Professional?

533 What year did Ron make his Worcestershire first-class debut?

534 Where did he make his West Indies Test debut?

535 He failed to score a century against only one County. Which County?

536 What year did he take his benefit?

537 What was unique about his last innings for Worcester-shire?

538 Which County did he join in 1975?

539 What was his highest innings for Worcestershire?

540 In how many Lord's one-day finals did he appear for Worcestershire?

541 Name his son who played in the 1987 'Cockspur' Cup final at Lord's.

2nd XI CHAMPIONSHIP – I

542 What year did Worcestershire enter the 2nd XI Championship?

543 When did they win their first Championship title?

544 Who captained them on most occasions in the early seasons?

545 Who has scored most runs for Worcestershire in a 2nd XI Championship career?

546 Who has taken most wickets for Worcestershire in a 2nd XI Championship career?

547 Who coached them to their first Championship title?

548 When did Worcestershire next win the 2nd XI Championship?

549 Which batsman has scored their highest individual innings?

550 Which bowler has the best bowling performance in an innings?

551 Which two openers had an unbeaten partnership of 286 in 1971?

NORMAN GIFFORD – I

552 He shares his birthplace with Stan Laurel of Laurel and Hardy fame, but where is this?

553 Who was the Worcestershire coach when he joined the County?

554 With which Birmingham League club did he play for on moving to Worcestershire?

555 He made his first-class debut in 1960. What was unusual about his first appearance?

556 Which other Worcestershire player was a colleague in the last Gentlemen v. Players match at Lord's in 1962?

557 In 1963 he joined Martin Horton, and in the role of 'night watchman' helped him add 108 for the second wicket, during which time Norman scored 89, his highest first-class innings. Who was this against?

558 In the first year of the Gillette Cup (1963) Norman won a 'Man of the Match' award. Where did he achieve this?

559 He made his Test debut against Australia at Lord's in 1964. Who was his captain in this match?

560 How many Test appearances did he make?

561 In 1965 he performed his only first-class hat-trick. Who were the opponents?

GILLETTE CUP (1963-80)

562 Who were the visitors for the first Gillette Cup match at New Road?

563 Who was 'Man of the Match'?

564 Who helped Tom Graveney add 145 for the third wicket in this match?

565 Worcestershire lost to Sussex in the first ever one-day final at Lord's, but whom did they beat in the semi-final?

566 Who scored Worcestershire's first century in this competition?

567 Who presented him with the 'Man of the Match' award?

568 Jack Flavell had a career average of 9.75 taking 33 wickets for 322 runs. Who is the only bowler in the history of the Gillette Cup to finish with a better average?

569 Worcestershire hold the Gillette Cup record for using the shortest number of overs in an innings (not including reduced-overs matches). Whom did they beat using only 10.1 overs, batting second?

570 Only one Worcestershire batsman has carried his bat through a completed 60 overs of a Gillette Cup match. This was against Lancashire in 1971 but who was the batsman?

571 Only 12 players appeared for three different Counties in the Gillette Cup. Name a Worcestershire player who was amongst this dozen.

572 Who scored the first century against Worcestershire?

573 Who were Worcestershire's first Minor County opponents?

574 Who helped Roy Booth add 21 runs for the last wicket in the 1963 final, a partnership that remained the tenth-wicket record at Lord's throughout the Gillette Cup finals?

575 In 1966 which Warwickshire-born bowler, playing for Hampshire, had an analysis of 12-1-89-0?

576 Who has Worcestershire's most economical Gillette Cup bowling analysis?

577 Worcestershire lost to Warwickshire in the 1966 final but who was 'Man of the Match'?

578 Who won most 'Man of the Match' awards for Worcestershire, sharing the record for the competition?

579 Which two Lancashire players share this achievement with him?

580 Roy Booth scored 55 against Notts in 1968. Who is the only other Worcestershire wicket-keeper to score a Gillette Cup half-century?

581 Who beat Worcestershire quite easily in their last Gillette Cup match?

582 Who is this early Worcestershire batsman who is much better known for his bowling?

583 Who is this Worcestershire captain?

584 Who is the visiting captain?

585 What Worcestershire record does he share with Graeme Hick?

586 He was the only Worcestershire representative on which infamous M.C.C. tour?

587 Which other Indian Test captain has played for Worcestershire?

588 Who is this Worcestershire batsman?

589 Who is taking the catch at first slip?

590 Who is the umpire?

591 Have a guess at the missing bowler at New Road in 1973.

592 Worcestershire v. the West Indies in 1950. Who is third from the right on the back row?

593 Who captained the West Indies in this rain-affected match?

ALAN ORMROD

594 Where was he born?
595 In 1972 he had his career best bowling figures. Who was this against?
596 Where did he score his highest first-class innings of 204* in 1973?
597 Who was his captain on the M.C.C. under-25 tour of Pakistan in 1966-67?
598 How many Benson and Hedges Gold Awards did he win?
599 How many centuries did he score for Worcestershire?
600 In 1980 he scored a century in each innings of a match at Worcester. Who were Worcestershire's opponents?
601 When did he take his benefit?
602 For which Birmingham League club did he play in his younger days?
603 When did he make his first-class debut?
604 Who was his opening partner during Worcestershire's only 200-run Sunday League partnership?
605 Where did this take place?
606 When did he begin to regularly open the innings with Glenn Turner?
607 How many times did he reach 1,000 runs in a season?
608 When did he join Lancashire?

NORMAN GIFFORD – 2

609 Which was the year of his benefit?
610 When did he become one of Wisden's 'Five Cricketers of the Year'?
611 During the winter of 1971-72 Norman went on a tour with a World XI. Where did they tour?
612 Which year was Norman part of a quartet of Worcestershire bowlers who each took over 100 first-class wickets during the season?
613 In 1968 he had his career-best bowling figures of 8-28. Who was this against?

614 Which year did he first captain Worcestershire at Lord's in a one-day final?

615 Only two players have made more first-class appearances for Worcestershire. Don Kenyon (589) is one, but who is the other?

616 When was he awarded the M.B.E.?

617 Norman toured India and Pakistan during the winter of 1972-73. Who was his captain?

618 Which was the year of his testimonial?

619 What award was he the first cricketer to receive and win again ten years later?

620 When did he become a Test Selector?

621 When Norman unwisely declared 148 runs behind in a match reduced to two days in 1979, which captain asked him to follow-on?

622 In 1980 Norman moved to second place behind Reg Perks (2,143) with most first-class career wickets for Worcestershire. Whom did he overtake?

623 When did he relinquish the captaincy to Glenn Turner?

2nd XI CHAMPIONSHIP – 2

624 What year did Worcestershire achieve their third title success?

625 Who captained them that season on most occasions?

626 What was unusual about the last and last-but-one appearance of T.W. Graveney in Worcestershire's 2nd XI Championship side?

627 Who scored the first century for Worcestershire in the 2nd XI Championship?

628 Who helped M.J. Weston add 385 for the fourth wicket v. Gloucestershire in 1984?

629 Who partnered M.G. Scothern in a last-wicket partnership of 109 v. Leicestershire in 1984?

630 Which bowler dismissed J. Lyon, J. Simmons and B.W. Reidy with consecutive deliveries at Bootle in 1972?

631 What year did Basil D'Oliveira first appear in the 2nd XI Championship for Worcestershire?

632 Who captained them in 1988?

633 What position were they in in the 1988 Championship table?

BASIL D'OLIVEIRA

634 Which Lancashire League club did Basil leave South Africa to join in 1960?

635 Who, besides John Arlott, helped Basil get this appointment?

636 Where did he make his first-class debut?

637 For which club in the Birmingham League did he play whilst qualifying for Worcestershire?

638 Against which touring side did he make his Worcestershire debut?

639 He made a century on his Championship debut against Essex, but who was the other batsman to share a 183-run partnership with him?

640 In 1966 Basil scored 101 out of a partnership of 107 at Worcester against Notts. Who was his 'sleeping partner'?

641 He scored a century on a Worcestershire tour abroad, but who was it against?

642 Against which country did he make his Test debut?

643 His best Worcestershire bowling figures are 6-29 (11-68 in the match) performed in 1968. Who were the opposition?

THE 1964 CHAMPIONSHIP YEAR

644 Whom did Worcestershire beat at Worcester to win the County Championship?

645 Who beat Warwickshire to make sure Worcestershire won the Championship?

646 Which batsman scored most runs and finished top of their averages?

647 And who took most wickets?

648 But who finished at the top of the bowling averages?

649 Which touring side visited Worcester at the end of April?

650 Which player made his first-class debut for Worcestershire in 1964?

651 Tom Graveney recorded his 100th hundred during the season, but who were Worcestershire's opponents?

652 Jim Standen finished top of the national bowling averages but which Worcestershire player finished second to him?

653 Worcestershire beat their nearest rivals Warwickshire at Edgbaston in July. Whose benefit match was this?

654 Who beat Worcestershire in the first round of the Gillette Cup?

655 Who inflicted the first Championship defeat of the season against Worcestershire?

656 The best Worcestershire bowling figures of the season were performed by Jack Flavell with 9-56 at Kidderminster. Who were the opponents?

657 Don Kenyon stood down from the matches against the Universities. Who took over the captaincy?

658 Roy Booth completed his 100th dismissal with the last wicket of the season taken by Worcestershire. Which batsman did he stump off Norman Gifford?

TOM GRAVENEY

659 When did he join the County from Gloucestershire?

660 For whom did he play in the Birmingham League during his qualifying period?

661 He scored 13,160 runs for Worcestershire averaging 46.17. Would you think that was more or less than his Gloucestershire aggregate?

662 He played in 31 Test Matches as a Worcestershire player, but how many altogether?

663 He was the last Worcestershire player to captain England in a Test Match. Who were the opposition?

664 How many centuries had he scored at the end of his career?

665 He had a benefit with Gloucestershire in 1959 but when did he have one with Worcestershire?

666 He won two Gillette Cup 'Man of the Match' awards, one of them for an innings of 61 not out in 1969. He finished, however on the losing side. Who were Worcestershire's opponents?

667 When was he officially appointed captain of Worcestershire?

668 He scored centuries for Worcestershire against every County bar three. Glamorgan and Lancashire were two of them, but which was the other?

THE 1965 CHAMPIONSHIP YEAR

669 Where did Worcestershire clinch the County Championship?

670 Worcestershire won by four wickets. Roy Booth was one of the not-out batsmen, but who was the other?

671 Which Hampshire Captain made a sporting declaration at Bournemouth when rain threatened to ruin the match?

672 Who scored a century on his Worcestershire County Championship debut?

673 During the season three bowlers performed the hat-trick. Len Coldwell and Norman Gifford were two of them, but who was the third?

674 Roy Booth missed three Championship matches. Who replaced him behind the stumps?

675 Who was President of the club during this centenary year?

676 Which touring side visited Worcester during the season?

677 Who scored most runs and finished top of Worcestershire's Championship averages?

678 Who took most wickets and finished top of Worcestershire's Championship averages?

679 Worcestershire received a bye in the first round of the Gillette Cup, but who beat them in the second round?

680 Which Leicestershire batsman scored a hundred in each innings of the match against Worcestershire at Grace Road?

681 How many consecutive matches did Worcestershire win at the end of the season?

682 Who, apart from Roy Booth, held most catches for Worcestershire during the Championship programme?

683 One of the 1964 heroes played in only one match in 1965. Who was he?

684 What year did he join the County?
685 With which Birmingham League club did he spend his qualifying period?
686 Where was he born?
687 How many times did he play for New Zealand?
688 How many times did he play for Worcestershire?
689 He scored ten centuries for Worcestershire in 1970. Whose club record did this break?
690 Against which County did he record his 100th hundred?
691 In which sport is his younger brother prominent?
692 How many 100s did he record for Worcestershire?
693 What was his highest innings score?

PICTURE QUIZ - 7

694 Who is this Worcestershire bowler with Kidderminster connections?

695 A group of young Worcestershire cricketers, but what was
the occasion?

696 Who were their opponents?

697 Which two players have since played Test cricket?

698 Who is on the far left of the front row?

699 Name Worcestershire's first Australian-born player.

700 Martin Horton receives the 'Man of the Match' award in 1966 for his efforts against Essex, but who is the presenter?

701 Jim Cumbes and Mike Vockins, but who is the gentleman on the right?

702 New Road scoreboard, but what was the occasion?

703 Name this Shropshire-born batsman.

704 Jim Laker at Alf Gover's Wandsworth Cricket School, but who is the young Worcestershire bowler?

JOHN PLAYER LEAGUE – I

705 The League began in 1969. Who were Worcestershire's first opponents?

706 Who scored their first century?

707 Who was their first bowler to take five wickets in an innings?

708 In which season did Worcestershire make the first ever innings total of over 300 runs?

709 Who were their opponents?

710 Four batsmen scored half-centuries in this innings. Turner, Ormrod and Imran Khan were three of them, but who was the fourth?

711 Who has scored most runs for Worcestershire in a Sunday League season?

712 Who was the first Worcestershire batsman to aggregate 1,000 runs?

713 Glenn Turner was the first Worcestershire batsman to win the BBC TV Fastest Televised Fifty Award. Who was this against?

714 Who has taken most wickets in a John Player season for Worcestershire?

1971 JOHN PLAYER LEAGUE

715 Whom did Worcestershire beat in their final match of the season?

716 Where did this take place?

717 Who beat Lancashire the following week to make sure Worcestershire won the League title?

718 Who scored most runs for Worcestershire in the League that season?

719 Vanburn Holder (32) took most wickets, but who came second with 20?

720 Who finished runners-up to Worcestershire?

721 And who finished last?

722 Worcestershire had four different captains in four consecutive matches. Gifford, Turner and Headley were three of them, but who was the fourth?

723 Why did Norman Gifford miss the last four League matches?

724 Which wicket-keeper made his Sunday League debut v. Gloucestershire?

725 Worcestershire won one of their away matches by just one run. Whom did they beat?

726 Which Hampshire bowler was hit for three sixes in his last two overs at Worcester with 34 runs coming from them?

727 One century was scored against Worcestershire during the season. Which Test all-rounder was responsible?

728 Which Staffordshire-born player made his Sunday League debut against Glamorgan?

729 Worcestershire lost only one match at home during the season and that took place at Dudley. Who were the visitors?

730 Who have beaten Worcestershire in both their Lord's finals?

731 Graham Johnson was 'Man of the Match' in 1976, but who took the award in 1973?

732 Who scored Worcestershire's first century in this competition?

733 Which Worcestershire cricketer played against them in the above match?

734 Who is the only Worcestershire bowler to have taken five wickets in an innings on three occasions?

735 Who won Worcestershire's first Gold Award in this competition?

736 And who won their last?

737 Who scored the first Benson and Hedges century against Worcestershire?

738 Only three Worcestershire batsmen have career runs exceeding 1,000. Glenn Turner (1,433) and Phil Neale (1,384) are two of them, but who is the third?

739 Who has taken the most wickets for Worcestershire in this competition?

GLENN TURNER - 2

740 How many runs did he aggregate for Worcestershire?

741 For three years after his retirement he was leading run-scorer in the Sunday League. What was his final aggregate?

742 Who eventually overtook him?

743 Against which County, in 1980, after a declaration, was he left 228 not not?

744 What was his highest Sunday League innings?

745 What year did he take his benefit?

746 When did he receive his County cap?

747 Where in 1973 did he score his 1,000th run by the end of May?

748 Which season was he County captain?

749 How many Benson and Hedges Gold Awards did he receive?

750 Where did Worcestershire win the County Championship?

751 Who scored most runs and also finished top of the batting averages?

752 Who took most wickets and also finished top of the bowling averages?

753 Two bowlers made their first-class debuts for Worcestershire during the season. One of them was Ravi Senghera, but who was the other?

754 Who were the tourists who visited Worcester in April?

755 And who were the tourists who came to Worcester in September only to find the match abandoned without a ball being bowled?

756 Skipper Norman Gifford only missed the Oxford University match at Oxford all season. Who captained in his absence?

757 Which 'night watchman' went in to bat on Saturday evening, and on Monday recorded his maiden century?

758 What were Norman Gifford's bowling figures at Chelmsford when Essex were bowled out for 84?

759 Worcestershire lost to the same County in the Benson and Hedges quarter-final, and also the Gillette semi-final. Name the County.

760 Which Worcestershire wicket-keeper took six catches in Hampshire's first innings at Portsmouth?

761 Which batsman scored a double century against Yorkshire, the first one ever by a Worcestershire batsman in Yorkshire?

762 Worcestershire were beaten twice during the season in two days, once at Portsmouth by Hampshire and once in July at Worcester. Who beat them at Worcester?

763 Who was the well-known Worcestershire character to lose his life in a car accident in August?

764 Two players who appeared in the successful Championship side left the staff at the end of the season. One was Bob Lanchbury, but who was the other?

765 Which fielder, other than a wicket-keeper, has taken most catches for Worcestershire in a season?

766 Which wicket-keeper has taken most catches for Worcestershire in a John Player season?

767 Only one player has scored a century and taken four wickets in the same match. Who is this Worcestershire all-rounder?

768 In 1976 against Warwickshire at Worcester two Worcestershire batsmen retired hurt. Basil D'Oliveira was one of them, but who was the other?

769 Glenn Turner hit ten sixes in the 1980 season, but who equalled this Worcestershire John Player record?

770 Who has the best bowling figures in a match for Worcestershire?

771 Who is the youngest Worcestershire batsman to score a John Player century?

772 Who is the youngest bowler to take five wickets for Worcestershire in the Sunday League?

773 Who has hit most sixes in a Sunday League innings for Worcestershire?

774 Worcestershire have won only one John Player match by ten wickets. Who were their opponents?

775 Who is the only Worcestershire wicket-keeper to win a Gold Award?

776 In 1975 Worcestershire lost one of their zonal games to a non-Championship side. Who were the opposition?

777 Who was Basil D'Oliveira's runner in the 1976 final after he had pulled a hamstring in the field earlier?

778 Two Worcestershire batsmen scored centuries at Old Trafford in 1980. Glenn Turner scored 122, but who scored 128?

779 Who was the captain who declared his side's innings closed after just one over?

780 Who took Somerset's place in the quarter-final when they were deservedly disqualified from the competition?

781 In 1975 Worcestershire lost all their zonal matches. Which other year did they repeat this performance?

782 Who are the only County that Worcestershire have not met in the Benson and Hedges Cup?

783 Worcestershire last reached the Benson and Hedges semi-finals in 1986, but to whom did they then lose by 11 runs at New Road?

784 Who is the only former Worcestershire player to gain the Gold Award when playing against them?

WINTER CRICKET EVENINGS

785 When did the first of these take place?

786 Who was the first organiser of these events?

787 Name the seven speakers who have captained their country in Test cricket.

788 Three groundsmen have entertained us over the years, two of them – Gordon Prosser and Richard Stevens – from New Road. Who was the third?

789 Who is the only lady speaker to have been guest speaker?

790 On one evening in 1986 Mike Vockins had to contend with three speakers in the same evening. Who were they?

791 Three Hampshire captains have been our guests, Richard Gilliat and, more recently, Mark Nicholas, are two of them, but who is the third?

792 When Mike Vockins' guest was Mike Vockins what was the topic?

793 There have been two video evenings, one being a re-run of Basil D'Oliveira's *This is Your Life*. What was the other?

794 Two appointed captains of Glamorgan have been subjected to the M.D.V. cross-examination. Wilf Wooller was one but who was the other?

795 Worcestershire 1986. Name the player on the extreme right of the back row.

796 Who are the two New Zealanders in the photograph?

797 Reg Perks leads out Worcestershire. What season was he the first professional to be appointed Captain of Worcestershire?

798 Who is at the top of the steps?

799 Doug Slade in 1963 toured with a Commonwealth side and played in three unofficial Tests, but in which country?

800 Against whom did Doug Slade score his only first-class century?

801 Who is this batsman who played just one first-class match for Worcestershire?

802 What was unusual about this match?

803 Who captained Worcestershire?

804 Who were Worcestershire's first opponents in this competition?

805 Glenn Turner scored Worcestershire's first Nat-West century. Where did this take place?

806 Worcestershire failed to beat first-class opposition until the competition was in its fifth year. Whom did they beat to end this run?

807 Who was 'Man of the Match'?

808 Who was the first former Worcestershire player to appear against them in the Nat-West Trophy?

809 Worcestershire have only visited one Minor County, having been drawn at home in all the other matches. Where did they go?

810 Who was 'Man of the Match'?

811 Which bowler in 1982 had taken the first four Yorkshire wickets when rain came with their score at 40-4 chasing 287, only for Yorkshire to win with three balls to spare the following day?

812 Phil Neale has captained Worcestershire in all but one of their Nat-West Trophy matches. Who was captain in this match?

813 Whose throw ran out Mike Gatting at Lord's in 1988?

814 Who has the best bowling figures against Worcestershire?

815 Who was the first Worcestershire bowler to take five wickets in a Nat-West Trophy match?

816 Which two Worcestershire batsmen scored centuries in the same innings in 1987?

817 Which Worcestershire player won two 'Man of the Match' awards in 1988?

818 Worcestershire reached the semi-final of the Nat-West Trophy for the first time in 1985. Who barred their way to their fifth Lord's final?

819 Where did the Supporters' Association coach go to, whilst Worcestershire were bowling out Glamorgan's first four batsmen when play eventually began just before six o'clock at Swansea in 1985?

820 Who is the only West Indian Test cricketer to have played for Worcestershire in the Nat-West Trophy?

821 Who has the best bowling figures for Worcestershire in this competition?

822 Who is the only Worcestershire batsman to be dismissed for 99 in the Nat-West Trophy?

823 Which batsman in 1988 scored a century, but failed to win the 'Man of the Match' award?

JOHN PLAYER LEAGUE – 3

824 Worcestershire have had three John Player League hat-tricks performed against them. Which Sussex bowler took the first of them?

825 What was unique about all of them?

826 They won the League in 1971, but which year were they runners-up to Hampshire?

827 Who has scored the highest individual innings for Worcestershire?

828 Who has scored the highest individual innings against them?

829 Who has the best bowling performance against Worcestershire?

830 What was unusual about Jim Cumbes' debut for Worcestershire in 1972?

831 Worcestershire won the Sunday League in 1971. Who were the 'wooden spoonists'?

832 Who has the highest aggregate of runs against Worcestershire?

833 Who has hit most Sunday League sixes in a career for Worcestershire?

834 When did he make his Worcestershire first-class debut?

835 He scored his first century in 1976 at Worcester. Who were the opposition?

836 Where did he score his first County Championship hundred?

837 He has taken one first-class wicket. Who was this solitary victim?

838 He took part in his first double-century partnership in 1979 at Worcester in the first innings against Notts and followed with another in the second innings. Who were his partners?

839 He made his Sunday League debut in a match that ended in a tie, with Philip and Norman Gifford the not-out batsmen at the finish. Who were the opposition?

840 Who was the manager of Lincoln City when Philip joined the soccer professionals?

841 Except for one match, all Phil's cricket has been played for Worcestershire. For whom did he play this one match?

842 He has scored one Sunday League century. Who were the opposition?

843 He shares the record Sunday League partnership of 68 for the Worcestershire ninth wicket. This took place at Bristol in 1980, but who was his partner?

844 Philip has been a victim in two Sunday League hat-tricks against Worcestershire. Colin Tunnicliffe at Derby in 1979 was the first bowler, but who in 1987 was the second?

845 At which university did Philip earn his honours degree in Russian?

846 For which minor County did he appear between 1972 and 1974?

847 When did Philip become the officially appointed captain of Worcestershire?

848 How many Benson and Hedges Gold Awards has he won?

849 Whom did Worcestershire beat to begin their successful season?

850 Who was the only Worcestershire player to make his Sunday League debut?

851 Ian Botham had his career-best Sunday League bowling figures of 5-27, but who was this against?

852 In their defeat at Trent Bridge, which bowler did the hat-trick against Worcestershire?

853 How many consecutive century partnerships did Tim Curtis and Ian Botham achieve?

854 Where did they begin?

855 Ian Botham hit a Worcestershire record of 14 Sunday League sixes during the season. The previous best had been ten shared by two batsmen. Glenn Turner was one, but who is the other?

856 Who scored most runs in the League during the season?

857 And who took most wickets?

858 Steven Rhodes took 24 dismissals, at that time a season's record for Worcestershire. Who held the record previously?

859 What was unusual about Richard Illingworth's only wicket against Warwickshire?

860 Who had the best Worcestershire bowling figures in the last match against Northants?

861 How many times did Worcestershire appear on BBC 2 *Grandstand* during the season?

862 Three players, who had previously played in the Sunday League with other Counties, made their Worcestershire debuts during the season. Botham and Dilley were two of them, but who is the other?

863 Who was the only batsman to score a century against Worcestershire in the League during the season?

864 Where did Graeme make his Worcestershire debut in 1984?

865 He batted at number nine scoring 82 not out, but with whom did he share an unbroken eighth-wicket partnership of 133?

866 He made his first-class debut for Zimbabwe in Harare in October 1983. Who were the opposition?

867 For which Birmingham League club did he score 1,234 runs in 1984?

868 Against which Birmingham League club did he score 182 not out, the highest innings since the Second World War?

869 How many centuries did he score in the Birmingham League?

870 Against whom did he score his first first-class century for Worcestershire?

871 In 1986 he scored double centuries in two consecutive innings. Who is the only other batsman to perform this feat for Worcestershire?

872 The first of these double centuries was scored at the age of 20 years and 46 days. Who was the previous youngest double centurion for Worcestershire?

873 In 1988 he was dismissed just once without scoring. Who was the bowler on this occasion?

874 For most of the season he topped the national batting averages, but who eventually put him in second place?

875 Graeme was involved in three partnerships in 1988 that broke Worcestershire records. Who was his sixth-wicket partner during the stand of 265 at Taunton?

876 Which former English Test cricketer shares his 23 May birthday and had cause to celebrate himself in 1988?

877 In 1986 Graeme became the youngest batsman to aggregate 2,000 runs in a season. Who previously held this distinction?

878 For whom has he played first-class cricket in New Zealand in the past two seasons?

879 Who took the season's first wicket for Worcestershire?
880 Who was the batsman?
881 Who helped Graeme Hick add 202 runs in Worcestershire's first innings of the season?
882 Who scored Worcestershire's first half-century in their defence of the Refuge Assurance League?
883 Who were the captains at the first ever four-day match at New Road?
884 Worcestershire lost their first home game at New Road in the Refuge Assurance League against Notts, but who top-scored for them?
885 Who took the diving catch on the boundary to dismiss Graeme Hick in this match, and had signed an autograph before his congratulatory colleagues reached him?
886 Who bowled the last over for Worcestershire with Notts needing eight to win?
887 During his innings of 405* Graeme Hick added 177 unbroken with Richard Illingworth for a County eighth-wicket record. Whose 74-year-old record was beaten?
888 Whom did Graeme Hick hit for six to reach his 400?

889 Where did Worcestershire lose their only away County Championship match?
890 Who dismissed Ian Botham at Taunton in the County Championship?
891 Only two century partnerships were recorded against Worcestershire all season in the County Championship, one of them being 105 for the third Warwickshire wicket by Asif Din and David Thorne at Worcester. Who were responsible for the other?
892 Who dismissed Tim Curtis at Old Trafford with his first ball in Sunday League cricket?

893 Somerset were beaten by seven wickets at Taunton in the Sunday League, but who said of his dismissal, 'It was a marvellous catch, one of the best I've been out to.'?

894 One of Worcestershire's Benson and Hedges zonal matches was abandoned without a ball being bowled, but at which venue?

895 But for an accident to the cricket square where should this match originally have taken place?

896 Worcestershire lost one of these zonal games, but who won the Gold Award?

897 Off one Benson and Hedges over during the zonal games, Phil Neale hit 28 runs. Who was the unfortunate bowler?

898 Which Worcestershire bowler had Benson and Hedges career-best figures during the season?

PICTURE QUIZ - 9

899 Worcestershire 1949. What was unusual about the captaincy that season?

900 Who is the medium-paced bowler standing second from the right?

901 Roy Booth, one of Worcestershire's many Yorkshire-born wicket-keepers, three of whom appeared for Yorkshire prior to moving south. Booth and Steve Rhodes are two of them, but who was the other?

902 Which of the three appeared for Yorkshire on the most occasions?

903 Which Yorkshire-born wicket-keeper joined Worcestershire from Essex?

904 One of two brothers who played for Worcestershire, but this
one made his name with another County. Name the
brothers.

905 Not an unusual sight at New Road, but who is pictured?
906 For which County is he groundsman?

907 For what reason is Jack Flavell being applauded to the wicket?

908 Who was his last victim?

909 Who is the player in the cap?

910 Who is standing to the right of the capped player?

1988 – 3

911 Which Worcestershire player made his first-class debut at Grace Road?

912 Who returned from Leicestershire for his first Championship match since 1985?

913 Worcestershire were beaten at New Road in the quarter-final of the Benson and Hedges Cup, but who won the Gold Award?

914 Who top-scored for Worcestershire?

915 Who scored most Benson and Hedges runs for Worcestershire during the season?

916 Who won the Benson and Hedges Cup?

917 Who won the Gold Award at Lord's?

918 Graeme Hick scored his first Sunday League century in May, but who were the opposition?

919 Who reached his 2,000 Sunday League runs aggregate at Grace Road and in his next League innings at Lord's struck Angus Fraser for only his second six in the competition?

920 Who hit the winning runs for Worcestershire in the Sunday League match at Leicester with just two balls to spare?

1988 – 4

921 Graeme Hick reached his 1,000th run on 28 May. Whom did he late-cut for four to reach 153 and become one of only eight batsmen ever to gain this achievement before the end of May?

922 During all this excitement, who was making his Worcestershire debut?

923 Paul Pridgeon topped the national Sunday League averages and twice took four wickets in an innings. Against which Counties did he have these match-winning performances?

924 At Taunton, Worcestershire scored 628-7. Worcestershire's highest first-class innings total is 633 recorded in 1906, but who were the opposition?

925 Ian Botham took one first-class wicket for Worcestershire during his injury-hit season. Who was the victim?

926 Who took four catches at first slip in the first innings of this match?

927 Who captained Middlesex against Worcestershire at Lord's?

928 In this match, Phil Newport had career-best figures of 8-52, but which Worcestershire batsman scored his second century for the County at Headquarters?

929 Hick and Curtis had two partnerships together of 250 plus, with 284 against the West Indies the better of them. Who were the visitors for the other of 276?

930 Which unusual Hampshire bowlers opened their attack in the second innings of the match at Worcester?

1988 – 5

931 Paul Bent made his Championship debut in 1988, but who were the opposition?

932 Who helped Phil Neale (91) add 123 for a record Worcestershire fifth-wicket Sunday League partnership at Knypersley against Derbyshire?

933 Steve Rhodes scored his maiden century at Derby on Monday morning, 20 June. What was his Saturday night not-out score?

934 The last Worcestershire wicket-keeper to score a century before Rhodes was David Humphries. Who were the opposition that day?

935 For the first time ever one could telephone for live commentary on Worcestershire cricket. What number would you dial?

936 Who would you expect to answer the call?

937 Which former Worcestershire player was in the Cumberland team for the first round of the Nat-West Trophy at Worcester?

938 Who just failed to score his first 60-over century in this match?

939 Who should have met Worcestershire at Hereford in the Sunday League match that was abandoned without a ball being bowled?

940 Who was dismissed three short of a Sunday League century at The Oval?

1988 – 6

941 Who helped Neal Radford (65) rescue the Worcestershire first innings at Trent Bridge?

942 Incredibly Notts collapsed to 47-8 in their first innings, but who in turn rescued them?

943 Who helped Graeme Hick (198) against Yorkshire add a record 205 for the Worcestershire seventh wicket?

944 Who took eight Worcestershire wickets in the Championship match at Folkestone?

945 Name the Northants Secretary-Manager who suggested that their match with Worcestershire be replayed following the Geoff Cook follow-on incident?

946 How many overs were left on that Monday evening when play was called off after T.C.C.B. intervention?

947 What kept Graham Dilley out of the Worcestershire side against Sussex at Kidderminster?

948 Who helped Phil Neale add 181 for the fifth wicket at Kidderminster?

949 What record did Steve Rhodes equal in this match?

950 Steve McEwan had career-best figures of 4-34 at Worcester, but who were the visitors?

How near can you get to naming the following County XIs?

951 The first first-class match at Worcester v. Yorkshire in 1899.

952 The last XI prior to the First World War in 1914 v. Derbyshire at Worcester.

953 The last XI prior to the Second World War in 1939 v. Notts at Worcester.

954 The first XI after this war in 1946 v. the Indian Tourists at Worcester.

955 The side who lost to Sussex in the first ever Gillette Cup final at Lord's in 1963.

956 The side that beat Sussex at Hove in 1965 to retain the County Cup Championship title.

957 The XI beaten by Kent at Lord's in the 1973 Benson and Hedges Cup final.

958 The XI at Chelmsford in 1974 that helped bring the County Championship pennant back to New Road.

959 The side beaten again by Kent in the 1976 Benson and Hedges Cup final.

960 The 1988 Refuge Assurance Cup final XI beaten by Lancashire at Edgbaston.

1988 – 7

961 Which of the Cowdrey brothers did David Leatherdale hit for a straight six at Folkestone during his match-winning Sunday League innings of 62 not out?

962 Which wicket-keeper made his Sunday League debut against Worcestershire at Worcester having played once for Worcestershire's Second XI in 1986?

963 Which Sussex batsman carried his bat through the 40 overs of the Sunday League match at New Road?

964 Who dismissed Alan Fordham of Northants at Worcester to collect his first first-class wicket?

965 Which two bowlers opened Worcestershire's attack against the West Indies?

966 Which batsman scored the highest individual innings against Worcestershire during the 1988 season?

967 Who was the 'Man of the Match' adjudicator in the Nat-West semi-final at Worcester?

968 Which Warwickshire bowler had career-best figures against Worcestershire at Edgbaston?

969 Which 17-year-old player made his first-class debut in this match?

970 Who chose Mark Ramprakash as 'Man of the Match' in the Nat-West final at Lord's?

1988 – 8

971 Ricardo Ellcock played against Somerset at Worcester in his first Championship match since 1986. When did he make his first-class debut?

972 Who made his maiden first-class century at Abergavenny?

973 Who recorded Worcestershire's only 'pair' of the season in this match?

974 On reaching 79 in his second innings of the match at Abergavenny, Graeme Hick achieved what distinction?

975 What was the Glamorgan score in their first innings of the Sunday League match at Swansea when rain intervened?

976 In the re-started match Graeme Hick hit a six into the Mumbles Road, but who was the unfortunate bowler?

977 Who made his Championship debut against Worcestershire at The Oval?

978 How many wickets did Neil Foster take in the match at New Road?

979 Who top-scored in Worcestershire's second innings of this match?

980 Graeme Hick hit nine Refuge Assurance League sixes during the season, but who was his nearest Worcestershire rival with five?

TIES

Benefits, celebrations and appeals. Answer the following questions on this selection of ties.

981 A club benefit appeal, but when?

982 Whose benefit and when?

983 To celebrate which
important occasion?

984 Whose benefit and when?

985 For what achievement?

986 Whose benefit and when?

987 To celebrate which important occasion?

988 For what occasion?

989 When did this category of Membership begin?

990 Whose benefit and when?

991 In which match did Phil Neale bowl 14 overs in one innings?

992 Who was voted Worcestershire's uncapped player of the year?

993 Whom did Worcestershire beat to go top of the Refuge Assurance League for the first time in the season, Middlesex having been top since 19 June?

994 Who received the Dick Lygon Award for his contributions to Worcestershire cricket on and off the field?

995 Who opened the batting with Andy Lloyd for Warwickshire in the County Championship match at Worcester?

996 Martin Weston scored 95* and took part in a last-wicket stand of 85 with which partner?

997 Who was 'Man of the Match' adjudicator in the first ever Refuge Assurance Cup match at Worcester?

998 Who took 4-23 for Worcestershire in this match?

999 Who top-scored for Middlesex?

1000 For which award did David Frith, editor of *Wisden Monthly*, make a presentation to one of the players during the Worcestershire v. Glamorgan match at New Road?

1001 Worcestershire won the Refuge Assurance League, comfortably defeating Warwickshire by ten wickets, but off whose bowling did Steve Rhodes complete an inspiring leg-side stumping?

1002 Who overtook Worcestershire during the last match of the season to win the Second XI Championship?

1003 Who was 'Man of the Match' in the Refuge Assurance Cup final at Edgbaston?

1004 Who was the adjudicator?

1005 Gordon Lord scored 101, his maiden century for Worcestershire, at Bristol. At the fall of which wicket was he out?

1006 Who was the not-out batsman?

1007 Two bowlers took ten wickets in this match at Bristol. David Graveney had match figures of 14-165, but who was the other?

1008 Who were the umpires confronted with the problem of the damaged wicket during the last match of the season at New Road?

1009 Who top-scored for Glamorgan in their second innings?

1010 At what time did Worcestershire become County Champions?

Answers

THE EARLY DAYS - 1

1 3 March, 1865
2 1899
3 Paul Foley
4 H.K. Foster
5 Yorkshire
6 Tom Straw
7 G.A. Wilson
8 W.L. Foster, 954 runs av. 41.48
9 Kent
10 Surrey

THE EARLY DAYS - 2

11 H.K. Foster in 1900
12 G.A. Wilson in 1900
13 E.G. Arnold in 1902
14 William Greenstock, 1899, born in South Africa
15 E.G. Arnold in 1899
16 Hampshire
17 Given out for 'obstructing the field'
18 G.E. Bromley-Martin
19 1907
20 South Africa in 1901

THE FOSTERS - 1

21 Henry Knollys b. 1873
22 Wilfred Lionel b. 1874
23 Reginald Erskine b. 1878
24 Basil Samuel b. 1882
25 Geoffrey Norman b. 1884
26 Maurice Kirshaw b. 1889
27 Neville John Acland b. 1890
28 Only player to have captained England at both games at senior level
29 H.K., father of C.K. b. 1904
30 J.W. Greenstock, son of Jessie

THE FOSTERS – 2

31 Rev. H. Foster, House Master at Malvern College
32 G.N.
33 H.K.
34 B.S.
35 M.K.
36 Oxford
37 Middlesex
38 Racquets
39 W.L.
40 M.K

NICKNAMES

41 A.P. Singleton
42 J. Cumbes
43 R.E. Foster
44 D.J. Humphries
45 H.H.I. Gibbons
46 G.J. Lord
47 J.B. Higgins
48 C.V. Tarbox
49 S.R. Lampitt
50 P.J. Newport

A WORCESTERSHIRE A-Z

51 **A** Sir G.E. Abell (1923-39)
52 **B** C.N. Boyns (1976-79)
53 **C** R.J. Crisp (1938)
54 **D** A.R. Duff (1960-61)
55 **E** W.H.B. Evans (1901)
56 **F** J. Fox (1929-33)
57 **G** 'Freddie' Grisewood (1908)
58 **H** J. Horton (1934-38)
59 **I** J.D. Inchmore (1973-86)
60 **J** I.N. Johnson (1972-75)
61 **K** R.C.M. Kimpton (1937-49)

62 **L** K. Lobban (1952-54)

63 **M** M.S.A. McEvoy (1983-84)

64 **N** M. Nichol (1928-34)

65 **O** L. Oakley (1935-48)

66 **P** C.H. Palmer (1938-49)

67 **Q** B.W. Quaife (1928-37)

68 **R** Edward Grantham Righton Jnr (1934-36)

69 **S** J.B. Sedgley (1959-61)

70 **T** Sir G.S. Tomkinson (1903-26)

71 **U** Thomas Umphrey Wells (1950)

72 **V** L.P. Vorster (1988)

73 **W** P.J. Whitcombe (1949-52)

74 **Y** T.J. Yardley (1967-75)

PICTURE QUIZ – I

75 All Saints

76 Glover's Needle

77 Wilfred Rhodes (left) and Sidney Barnes

78 Lancashire in 1980

79 Hampshire

80 The Australians, captained by Syd Gregory, in a rain-affected drawn match

81 Batsmen: Duncan Fearnley and Tom Graveney. Wicket-keeper: Barrie Meyer. Bowler: Mike Procter. Umpire: Fred Jakeman

82 Left to Right: Ted Hemsley, Duncan Fearnley, Alan Ormrod, Doug Slade, Glenn Turner (his first first-team appearance for the County), Keith Baylis and Jim Standen

83 Roy Barker

84 Rodney Cass

85 John Elliott (second from left), Basil D'Oliveira (fifth from left), and Joe Lister (second from right)

FAMILY LINKS – I

86 Eddie and Fred Cooper

87 P.I. Pocock

88 Peter and 'Dick' Richardson
89 Peter Robinson
90 G.E. and E.G. Bromley-Martin
91 G.F. Wheldon and grandson J.W. Spilsbury
92 M.F.S. and A.N. Jewell (brothers) and J.M.H. Jewell (nephew)
93 A.W. and J.E.V. Isaac
94 S.J. Rhodes and W.E. Rhodes
95 E.J.O. and C.R. Hemsley

AUTOGRAPHS - I

96 Paul Fisher
97 Len Coldwell
98 Roy Booth
99 Dick Richardson
100 Rodney Cass
101 Alan Ormrod
102 Bob Carter
103 Don Kenyon
104 Charlie Palmer
105 Dipak Patel

AUTOGRAPHS - 2

106 Syd Buller
107 Bob Berry
108 Younis Ahmed
109 Collis King
110 Mark Scott
111 Cyril Walters
112 Jack Birkenshaw
113 Vanburn Holder
114 Brian Brain
115 Fred Rumsey

SURNAMES – I

116 Ponsonby
117 Graveney
118 Buller
119 Jackson
120 Bird
121 Johnson
122 Smith
123 Flavell
124 Baylis
125 McEvoy

ALL-ROUNDERS

126 M.J. Horton, 1961
127 S.H Martin
128 W.B. Burns v. Gloucestershire, 1913
129 B.L. D'Oliveira
130 J.D. Inchmore
131 D.N. Patel v. Northants, 1983
132 J.A. Cuffe, 1911
133 R. Howorth, 10,538 runs and 1,274 wickets
134 E.G. Arnold v. Warwickshire, 1909
135 Imran Khan v. Lancashire, 1976

ANAGRAMS

136 Younis Ahmed
137 Michael Vockins
138 Alexander Singleton
139 Keith Wilkinson
140 Basil D'Oliveira
141 Geoffrey Foster
142 Paul Pridgeon

143 Leonard Coldwell
144 Norman Whiting
145 Harry Moule

NEW ROAD, WORCESTER – I

146 The London County in 1899
147 Zimbabwe
148 George Platt
149 June 1951
150 Hereford
151 Revd George William Gillingham
152 Mr G.W. Nicholls
153 Brigadier M.A. Green, C.B.E., M.C.
154 1954
155 Bob Brookes

THE TWENTIES

156 Four – 1922, '26, '27 and '28
157 Fourteenth in 1921 and 1924
158 M.F.S. Jewell
159 M.K. Foster, 6,289 runs av. 30.09
160 Fred Root, 1,090 wickets av. 20.41
161 A.N. Jewell, brother of Captain M.F.S. Jewell
162 J.C. 'Farmer' White who took 218 Worcestershire wickets at an average of 11.41 during his career
163 W.V. Fox and L.G. Crawley
164 They were found lacking in the residential qualifications necessary to play for Worcestershire. Crawley moved to Essex and Fox spent two years with Dudley in the Birmingham League before returning in 1926
165 George Gunn

FRED ROOT

166 Derbyshire, at Somercotes, 1890
167 1921

168 Dudley
169 Three
170 Leg Theory (in swing bowling to usually seven fielders on the leg-side)
171 1925, 207 av. 17.52
172 F.S.G. Calthorpe to West Indies
173 Lancashire at Worcester, 1931
174 1928, 1,044 runs and 118 wickets
175 Todmorden

PICTURE QUIZ - 2

176 J.R. Ashman
177 Yes, Ashman played one match for Yorkshire v. Surrey in 1951
178 David Banks v. Oxford University, 1983
179 Bournville
180 Liam Botham
181 Simon Kimber (Sussex)
182 Left to Right – Glenn Turner, Henry Horton, Greg Watson and Norman Gifford
183 New South Wales
184 Hampshire
185 Dudley in 1914

SURNAMES - 2

186 Smith
187 Rumsey
188 Taylor
189 King
190 Wilcock
191 Tarbox
192 Broadbent
193 Warner
194 Fearnley
195 Fox

WICKET-KEEPERS

196 A.G. Pawson (1908), his son being H.A. (Tony)
197 C.B. Ponsonby (1927)
198 J.T. Murray (Middlesex)
199 B.W. Quaife, son of William 'George' Quaife
200 S.W. Styler
201 F.T. Summers
202 C.R.N. Maxwell
203 Syd Buller
204 Broughty Ferry, Dundee against Scotland
205 1960
206 P.B. Fisher
207 G.R. Cass
208 D.J. Humphries
209 J.F. Maclean
210 J.C. Scholey

FOOTBALLING CRICKETERS

211 Jim Standen (West Ham)
212 Middlesbrough
213 Vic Fox
214 Doncaster Rovers
215 G.F. Wheldon (Aston Villa)
216 1974-75 League Cup v. Norwich City
217 A.J. Conway v. Gloucestershire at Moreton-in-Marsh, 1914
218 Blackburn Rovers
219 G.F. Wheldon
220 Len Beel

STOURBRIDGE

221 1905, beating Leicestershire by an innings and 207 runs
222 F.L. Bowley (217)

223 235 for the tenth wicket by Frank Woolley and Arthur
    Fielder for Kent in 1909
224 'Dick' Pearson
225 Glamorgan
226 Glenn Turner (161 and 101) v. Northants in 1981
227 Paul Pridgeon, Phil Neale, Tim Curtis and Mark Scott
228 Jim Yardley (past) and Kapil Dev (future), although Tim
    Lamb did speak at one of our winter cricket evenings
229 Len Hutton
230 Charles Lyttleton with 48
231 Mike Rowley, the scorer for Stourbridge C.C.
232 Glamorgan, losing by 28 runs, in 1969
233 Cliff Gladwin, 7-43 and 9-41
234 Leicestershire
235 Roger Tolchard

'DOC' GIBBONS

236 Harold, Harry, Ian
237 On arriving at Worcester he carried his cricket gear in a little
    black Gladstone bag, like a doctor's bag
238 1927
239 Dudley
240 For the North against the South at Bournemouth, 1928
241 44
242 Northants
243 Kidderminster, v. Warwickshire 1934, v. Lancashire 1935
244 1934
245 Hampshire (111* and 100*) at Worcester
246 T.C. Lowry's New Zealanders, 2-27 and 1-68
247 Both were scored before lunch on consecutive days: 140 v.
    Kent, 18 May and 100 v. Hampshire, 19 May 1928
248 Vic Fox
249 Chelmsford
250 Advertising, eventually becoming President of the West
    Midlands Newspapers Advertising Association

BOOKS

251 Umpire Frank Chester
252 Basil D'Oliveira
253 The Association of Cricket Statisticians
254 Pat Murphy
255 Fred Root
256 1965
257 Roy Genders
258 W.R. Chignell
259 *Swings and Roundabouts*
260 M.D. Vockins

NEW ROAD – 2

261 C.F. Walters
262 The 1974 Test Trial
263 Geoff Boycott
264 Bill Faithfull
265 Gordon Prosser in 1972, 1973 and 1975
266 1971, October
267 Kidderminster
268 1956
269 The freehold of the County ground from the Dean and Chapter of Worcester Cathedral
270 Tom Langford

TO WORCESTERSHIRE FROM . . .

271 Gloucestershire
272 Kent
273 Essex
274 Middlesex
275 Warwickshire
276 Derbyshire
277 Lancashire
278 Lancashire
279 Warwickshire
280 Yorkshire

281 Derbyshire
282 Essex
283 Glamorgan
284 Hampshire
285 Lancashire
286 Gloucestershire
287 Northants
288 Kent
289 Sussex
290 Gloucestershire

PICTURE QUIZ – 3

291 Hagley Hall, home of C.J. Lyttleton, later the tenth Viscount Cobham
292 A.P. Singleton
293 B.P. King for Lancashire
294 L. Oakley (extreme left insert) and R.D.M. Evers (extreme right insert)
295 P.F. Jackson (Scotland), S.H. Martin (South Africa) and F.B.T. Warne (Australia); third, fourth and fifth from the left on the back row
296 R.H.C. Human, born in Newcastle upon Tyne (second from right, middle row)
297 G.F. Wheldon
298 First time four Worcestershire bowlers had taken 100 wickets in a season:– left to right – Perks (139), Howorth (105), Jackson (102), Martin (114) in 1937. Equalled in 1961 by Flavell (158), Coldwell (140), Gifford (133) and M.J. Horton (101)
299 Fred Root
300 Belfast, Worcestershire's only Irish-born cricketer
301 Paul Terry (Hampshire)

TEST MATCH SPECIALS

302 The Nawab of Pataudi
303 Victor Trumper caught by R.E. Foster
304 P.E. Richardson
305 R.E. Foster
306 C.F. Root
307 R. Howorth
308 A.G. Archer (England v. South Africa, 1898-99)
309 R.G.A. Headley (West Indies v. England, 1973)
310 R.T.D. Perks
311 G.H.T. Simpson-Hayward
312 Frank Chester
313 R.T.D. Perks
314 Durban, South Africa
315 C.H. Palmer
316 The Nawab of Pataudi

REG PERKS

317 1930
318 Walter Hammond
319 West Indies at The Oval in 1939
320 Warwickshire at Edgbaston in 1933
321 Jack Hobbs caught by George Brook at The Oval
322 Cyril Walters
323 2,143 av. 23.73
324 Somerset
325 81 against Notts
326 1955

THE THIRTIES

327 1932
328 C.C. Dacre and W.R. Hammond
329 Chelmsford

330 C.F. Walters

331 Len Hutton with 196 for Yorkshire

332 Alf Gover (Surrey)

333 Yorkshire

334 Jack Mercer (Glamorgan), who until 1983 was the Northants scorer

335 R.C.M. Kimpton (1937) following the Nawab of Pataudi (1931-33)

336 T.W.J. Goddard for Gloucestershire with 7-84 and 6-109 at Dudley and 6-68 and 10-113 at Cheltenham

337 This was the only season of the eight-ball over in English cricket

338 Charlie Bull

339 Dick Howorth having Harold Butler (Notts) caught by Charles Lyttleton

340 'Doc' Gibbons, 17,200 av. 35.90

341 Reg Perks, 1,063 av. 22.70

DUDLEY - I

342 1911

343 Gloucestershire, captained by Gilbert Jessop

344 Tom Hayward (Surrey), 182 in 1912

345 F.R. Foster (Warwickshire)

346 C.C. Dacre

347 P.F. Jackson, 9-45 v. Somerset, 1935

348 R.E.S. Wyatt,104 (1925), 129* (1929) and 187* (1933) for Warwickshire

349 7-13 July 1951

350 'Roly' Jenkins

351 T.L. Pritchard for Warwickshire

DUDLEY - 2

352 J.D. Inchmore, 4-9 v. Northants

353 G.M. Turner, 121 v. Sussex, 1972

354 J.C.J. Dye (Northants)
355 C.W.L. Parker (5-40 and 5.38), 1924
356 B.L. D'Oliveira, 107 v. Kent, 1965
357 Peter Stimpson v. Sussex
358 D.L. Acfield (Essex), 5-28 in 1976
359 1971
360 Yorkshire
361 Notts

DICK HOWORTH

362 1933
363 Lancashire
364 Old Hill
365 India in 1946
366 D.V. Dyer, caught by Cliff Gladwin
367 G.O. Allen
368 West Indies, 1947-48
369 Warwickshire at Edgbaston
370 Three in 1938, 1939 and 1946
371 1951

UNUSUAL VENUES

372 Cowes, Isle of Wight, against Hampshire in 1956 and 1962
373 v. Notts at Cleethorpes
374 Knypersley v. Derbyshire in 1985 and 1988
375 Chichester, and the Sussex brothers were John and James
    Langridge and Charlie and Jack Oakes
376 Harlow
377 Middlesbrough, 1978
378 Lydney against Gloucestershire (5-26)
379 Nelson
380 Glasgow, Worcestershire beating Scotland by two wickets in
    1986
381 Peterborough

382 Guildford

383 15-87, A.J. Conway at Moreton-in-Marsh v. Gloucestershire in 1914

384 Blackburn

385 Wells, Somerset

386 Byfleet v. Surrey

387 Hertfordshire at Hitchin, 1985

388 Basingstoke, Hampshire

389 Dewsbury in 1901 and 1912

390 Pontypridd

391 Wellington, Worcestershire beating the Minor Counties by
97 runs

PICTURE QUIZ 4

392 Sussex in the Nat-West semi-final of 1986

393 Middlesex, who won by nine wickets

394 Alan Warner is at Derbyshire

395 D.N.F. Slade, 1,407 in 1978

396 Gilbert Parkhouse, the coach, on the extreme right of the
back row, who played seven Tests as a Glamorgan batsman

397 Len Beel (fifth from the left), Ted Hemsley (eighth from the
left) and Jim Standen (second from the left, front row)

398 For Somerset in 1969 against Warwickshire at Edgbaston

KIDDERMINSTER

399 Glamorgan

400 M.F.S. Jewell

401 1973, with the visit of Northants

402 W.E. Bates (Warwickshire), 1927

403 Essex

404 Derbyshire, on eight occasions

405 Chris Scott (Notts)

406 All three were caught by wicket-keeper George Dawkes

407 Middlesex

408 1969
409 Don Kenyon, 259 v. Yorkshire, 1956
410 Jack Flavell, 9-56 v. Middlesex, 1964
411 Somerset
412 Colin Cowdrey (Kent)
413 P.J. Newport

'ROLY' JENKINS

414 1938
415 1958
416 Nine
417 109 v. Notts at Trent Bridge, 1948
418 Twice, 1949 and 1952
419 1949
420 Alec Bedser
421 F.G. Mann (Middlesex)
422 113 v. Somerset, av. 21.07
423 West Bromwich, Dartmouth

DON KENYON - I

424 The Combined Services
425 Nigel Howard
426 Stourbridge
427 1959
428 70
429 1967
430 Ron Headley
431 Colwyn Bay
432 Eight
433 Middlesex

THE FORTIES

434 'Laddie' Outschoorn v. Northants at Worcester in August
     1949
435 George Dews

436 Lieutenant Michael Ainsworth
437 He only scored 107 instead of his usual double century!
438 Three – 236 (1930), 206 (1934) and 258 (1938)
439 Arthur Morris, 138
440 Peter Jackson
441 1949
442 Charlie Palmer
443 R.C.M. Kimpton v. Notts, at Stourbridge in 1949
444 First to aggregate 100 dismissals in a season
445 Dick Howorth
446 Allan White
447 Eddie Cooper, 5,676 av. 34.40
448 Dick Howorth, 445 av. 18.80

THE RICHARDSONS

449 Hereford
450 1952 v. Oxford University on the occasion of Dick's first-class debut for Worcestershire
451 Warwickshire
452 Peter, an amateur, playing for the Gentlemen, and Dick, a professional, for the Players
453 Kent 162, Worcestershire 161
454 1967
455 Stourbridge
456 65
457 1956, on the retirement of Reg Perks
458 The only four cricketers to appear for both Gentlemen and Players this century

LEN COLDWELL

459 Devon (1953-54) – the County of his birth
460 1955
461 1,029 av. 20.88
462 Keith Fletcher (Essex) at Brentwood, 1965

463 Surrey

464 Seven

465 Ted Dexter

466 The 1964 Australians

467 1968

468 Eric Bedser

DON KENYON – 2

469 Tom Graveney

470 March 1986

471 Stourbridge and District

472 India, Pakistan and Ceylon

473 A Test Selector

474 None

475 2,587 av. 40.42 v. Essex

476 Kidderminster

477 259

478 Wordsley, Staffs

WINTER EMPLOYMENT

479 Northern Districts

480 Boland

481 Tasmania

482 Northern Transvaal

483 Jamaica

484 South Africa for Natal in 1985/86 season

485 Barbados, debut 1966/67

486 J.B. 'Bunny' Higgins

487 Sri Lanka on tour with Zimbabwe 1983/84

488 Queensland

489 M.S.A. McEvoy
490 Not a player but the club, organised by the Friends of Worcestershire Cricket
491 Peter Moores for Sussex
492 Bob Berry
493 Derbyshire
494 G.H. Chesterton (Oxford blue 1949) second from left front row
495 Glamorgan
496 Kidderminster
497 Evesham
498 Gloucestershire beating them by six wickets
499 Eddie Cooper (122) for Worcestershire
500 Cedric Boyns
501 George Sharp for Northants at Milton Keynes

JACK FLAVELL

502 Wall Heath, Staffordshire
503 Walsall
504 Full back
505 1961 v. Australia
506 Four
507 1,507
508 At Dudley in 1959, 54 v. Warwickshire
509 9-30 v. Kent, 1955
510 Three
511 All lbw v. Lancashire, 1963
512 Himley
513 1961 with 171 wickets, av. 17.79
514 1965
515 1967
516 'The Rafters'

THE FIFTIES

517 H.K. Foster, former captain and scorer of 15,053 runs for the County
518 'Roly' Jenkins
519 Noman Whiting
520 Louis Devereux
521 Reg Simpson
522 Bob Wyatt
523 Charlie Palmer for Leicestershire
524 Michael Passey, aged 16 years 63 days, caught by Jim Pleass off Len Muncer for one
525 Ron Jones, aged 16 years 286 days
526 Hugo Yarnold, 14* in the second
527 Beat them by 117 runs, their only defeat other than Test Matches
528 Colin McCool, but, 'How many?' said Bill Alley
529 Derek Pearson and John Aldridge
530 20,087 av. 41.6
531 'Roly' Jenkins, 719 av. 23.30

RON HEADLEY

532 Dudley
533 1958
534 The Oval
535 Nottinghamshire
536 1972
537 He scored 112* v. Kent at Worcestershire in a Sunday League match
538 Derbyshire
539 187 v. Northants in 1971
540 Two – 1963 (Gillette) and 1973 (Benson and Hedges)
541 Dean

2nd XI CHAMPIONSHIP – I

542 1959

543 1962

544 J. Lister

545 C.D. Fearnley – 6,145 av. 39.14

546 R.G.M. Carter – 350 av. 18.94

547 C. Hallows

548 1963

549 M.J. Weston – 205* v. Gloucestershire, 1984

550 C.P. Roberts – 8-13 v. Lancashire, 1974

551 P.J. Stimpson and D.E.R. Stewart v. Glamorgan, 1971

NORMAN GIFFORD – I

552 Ulverston, Lancashire

553 Charlie Hallows

554 Dudley

555 Worcestershire lost to Kent at Tunbridge Wells by an innings in only one day's play

556 Tom Graveney

557 Oxford University at Oxford

558 He was the first 'Man of the Match' in a one-day final at Lord's

559 Ted Dexter

560 15

561 Derbyshire at Chesterfield

GILLETTE CUP (1963-80)

562 Surrey

563 Jim Standen with 5-14 and 13 not out

564 Ron Headley

565 Lancashire

566 Martin Horton v. Hampshire at Worcester, 1966

567 Peter May

568 Joel Garner with 32 wickets for 308 runs av. 9.62

569 Lancashire in 1963 by nine wickets at 2.20 p.m.

570 Glenn Turner 117* out of 215-6

571 Rodney Cass having played for Essex (1966-67), Worcester-
    shire (1969-75) and Shropshire (1976-78)
572 M.J. Procter (Gloucestershire), 101 in the 1973 semi-final at
    Worcester
573 Durham in 1968 Worcestershire winning by 16 runs after
    being bowled out for 98 runs, their lowest score
574 Bob Carter
575 D.W. 'Butch' White at Worcester
576 1972, N. Gifford 12-7-7-4 v. Surrey at Worcester
577 Bob Barber (Warwickshire)
578 Basil D'Oliveira, six
579 Clive Lloyd and Barry Wood
580 David Humphries 58 v. Glamorgan, Worcester, 1977
581 Middlesex, by ten wickets at Worcester in 1980

PICTURE QUIZ – 6

582 G.A. Wilson
583 A.P. Singleton
584 The Nawab of Pataudi (India, 1946)
585 Only Worcestershire batsmen to score two consecutive
    double centuries
586 D.R. Jardine's 'body line' series of 1932-33 in Australia
587 Kapil Dev
588 George Dews
589 Jim Yardley
590 Sam Cook
591 Brian Brain
592 Norman Whiting
593 John Goddard

ALAN ORMROD

594 Ramsbottom, Lancashire
595 Gloucestershire, 5-27 at Bristol
596 Dartford

597 Mike Brearley
598 Four
599 31
600 Somerset
601 1977
602 Dudley
603 1962
604 Dipak Patel
605 Southampton
606 1975
607 12
608 1984

NORMAN GIFFORD – 2

609 1974
610 1975
611 Australia
612 1961, along with Flavell, Coldwell and Horton
613 Yorkshire
614 1973, losing to Kent by 39 runs in the Benson and Hedges Cup
615 Reg Perks (561) with Gifford (528)
616 June 1978
617 Tony Lewis
618 1981
619 The Dick Lygon Award (1970 and 1980) for Worcestershire's best team man on and off the field
620 1982
621 P.J. Watts (Northants) at Worcester
622 Jack Flavell (1,507) and Norman's final Worcestershire total was 1,615 wickets
623 1981

2nd XI CHAMPIONSHIP – 2

624 1982
625 V.A. Holder (seven)

626 His last appearance was in July 1978, and his last but one was in August 1961
627 R.G.A. Headley, 129 v. Sussex, 1959
628 G.A. Hick
629 R.M. Ellcock
630 A.P. Pridgeon
631 1964 – scoring 0 v. Somerset
632 M.S. Scott
633 Runners-up

BASIL D'OLIVEIRA

634 Middleton
635 John Kay
636 Northern Rhodesia, for an International XI in 1962
637 Kidderminster
638 The 1964 Australians
639 Tom Graveney
640 For the eighth wicket with Brian Brain
641 101 v. a Jamaican Invitation XI at Montego Bay in 1966
642 The West Indies at Lord's 1966
643 Hampshire, at Portsmouth

THE 1964 CHAMPIONSHIP YEAR

644 Gloucestershire
645 Hampshire
646 Tom Graveney (2,271 runs av. 55.39)
647 Jack Flavell (101 av. 15.08)
648 Jim Standen (52 wickets av. 14.42)
649 Bobby Simpson's Australians
650 Basil D'Oliveira
651 Northants at Worcester
652 Len Coldwell
653 Jack Bannister
654 Glamorgan

655 Somerset at Worcester
656 Middlesex
657 Martin Horton
658 Ken Graveney, brother of Tom

TOM GRAVENEY

659 1961
660 Dudley
661 Less – he scored 19,705 av. 43.02 for Gloucestershire
662 79
663 Australia, at Leeds in 1968
664 122
665 1969
666 Derbyshire at Derby
667 1968
668 His former County, Gloucestershire

THE 1965 CHAMPIONSHIP YEAR

669 At Hove
670 Doug Slade
671 A.C.D. Ingleby-MacKenzie
672 Basil D'Oliveira (106 v. Essex)
673 Bob Carter v. Lancashire
674 John Elliot
675 Sir George Dowty
676 John Reid's New Zealanders
677 Tom Graveney (1,684 av. 48.11)
678 Jack Flavell (132 av. 14.99)
679 Sussex at Worcester
680 M.R. Hallam (107* and 149*)
681 Seven
682 Basil D'Oliveira, with 39
683 Jim Standen

GLENN TURNER - I

684 1967

685 Stourbridge

686 Dunedin, New Zealand

687 41

688 284

689 C.F. Walters

690 Warwickshire

691 Golf

692 72

693 311*

PICTURE QUIZ - 7

694 Ken Lobban

695 Final of the Warwick Under-25 Competition at Edgbaston, 1983

696 Leicestershire, who won with scores level but having lost fewer wickets

697 Phil Newport (fourth from left, back row, for England) and Greg Matthews (second from right, front row, for Australia)

698 Steve Watkins

699 J.A. Cuffe

700 Herbert Sutcliffe (Yorkshire and England)

701 Wing-Commander W.H.N. Shakespeare O.B.E., M.C., A.F.C., President of the County at the time of his death

702 Graeme Hick (172) and Tim Curtis (78) v. the West Indies, 1988, on the day that Graeme reached his 1,000 runs before the end of May

703 Barry Jones

704 Martin Horton

JOHN PLAYER LEAGUE - I

705 Surrey at The Oval, losing by five runs

706 G.M. Turner v. Sussex at Dudley, 1972

707 R.G.M. Carter v. Sussex at Hove, 1971

708 1975

709 Derbyshire

710 T.J. Yardley

711 Younis Ahmed, with 668 in 1979

712 R.G.A. Headley in 1970, after 40 innings

713 Northants off 32 balls at Worcester in 1972

714 V.A. Holder, 32 in 1971, av. 12.19

1971 JOHN PLAYER LEAGUE

715 Warwickshire

716 Dudley

717 Glamorgan

718 Ron Headley (554)

719 Bob Carter

720 Essex

721 Warwickshire

722 Basil D'Oliveira

723 He fractured his thumb in the second Test v. India at Old Trafford

724 Gordon Wilcock

725 Sussex at Hove

726 Bob Cottam

727 Gary Sobers at Newark

728 Keith Wilkinson

729 Northants

BENSON AND HEDGES CUP – 1

730 Kent, 1973 and 1976

731 Asif Iqbal

732 Ron Headley, 132 v. Oxford University at Worcester, 1973

733 Imran Khan, scoring 25 and taking 2-29

734 Norman Gifford

735 Glenn Turner v. Cambridge University, 1972

736 Phil Neale v. Yorkshire, 1988
737 Chris Balderstone, 100* for Leicestershire at Grace Road, 1976
738 Alan Ormrod with 1,587
739 John Inchmore, 71 av. 25.50 at 3.458 runs per over

GLENN TURNER – 2

740 22,298 av. 52.09
741 6,144 av. 37.46
742 D.L. Amiss
743 Gloucestershire
744 147 v. Sussex at Horsham, 1980
745 1978 (£21,103)
746 1968
747 Northampton
748 1981
749 Five

THE 1974 CHAMPIONSHIP SEASON

750 Chelmsford
751 Glenn Turner (1,098 av. 54.90)
752 Vanburn Holder (87 av. 15.60)
753 Paul Roberts
754 India
755 Pakistan
756 Ted Hemsley
757 John Inchmore v. Essex at Worcester
758 14 overs, seven maidens, 15 runs, seven wickets
759 Lancashire
760 Gordon Wilcock
761 Basil D'Oliveira
762 Leicestershire
763 Hugo Yarnold
764 Ron Headley

JOHN PLAYER LEAGUE – 2

765 G.M. Turner, 14 in 1979

766 D.J. Humphries, 19 in 1978

767 D.N. Patel (125 and 4-39) v. Hampshire at Southampton in 1982

768 Norman Gifford

769 Collis King

770 Paul Pridgeon, 6-26 v. Surrey at Worcester, 1978

771 M.J. Weston (23 years 108 days), 109 v. Somerset at Taunton, 1982

772 R.K. Illingworth (20 years 12 days), 5-24 v. Somerset at Worcester, 1983

773 G.M. Turner, seven v. Sussex at Horsham, 1980

774 Surrey, at Worcester, 1976

BENSON AND HEDGES CUP – 2

775 Steve Rhodes v. Warwickshire at Edgbaston, 1987

776 The Combined Universities at Fenners, by 66 runs

777 Glenn Turner

778 Phil Neale

779 Brian Rose for Somerset, at New Road in 1979

780 Glamorgan

781 1981

782 Sussex

783 Kent

784 David Smith (Surrey) for his 110* at The Oval in 1987

WINTER CRICKET EVENINGS

785 The autumn of 1972

786 Dick Thomas

787 George Mann, Donald Carr, Colin Cowdrey, Mike Smith, Tom Graveney and Glenn Turner

788 Bernard Flack (Edgbaston)

789 Jill Cruwys (English Ladies)
790 Graeme Hick, Steve Rhodes and Martin Weston
791 Nick Pocock
792 The English Counties XI tour of Zimbabwe in 1984-85, managed by the Speaker
793 A showing of *Benson and Hedges Golden Greats*
794 Malcolm Nash

PICTURE QUIZ – 8

795 Lawrence Smith
796 S.A. Thomson (extreme left, back row) and B.J. Barrett (sixth from left, back row)
797 1955
798 'Roly' Jenkins
799 Pakistan
800 Leicestershire, 1969
801 H.V. Patel, in 1985
802 Worcestershire included seven first-class debutants against Cambridge University
803 David Humphries

NAT-WEST TROPHY (1981-88)

804 Derbyshire at Worcester, losing by four wickets
805 At Headingley, 1982
806 Lancashire, by 14 runs at Old Trafford in 1985
807 Clive Lloyd (91), although David Smith scored 109 for Worcestershire
808 Younis Ahmed for Glamorgan, at Swansea in 1985
809 To Hitchin in 1985 to beat Hertfordshire, but will visit Cambridgeshire in 1989
810 Scots-born E.P. Neale for Herts
811 John Inchmore
812 Glenn Turner v. Derbyshire in 1981
813 Steve O'Shaughnessy

814 N.A. Mallender (Northants), 7-37 at Northampton in 1984
815 Kapil Dev, 5-52 v. Lancashire, 1985
816 Graeme Hick (172*) and Ian Botham (101) v. Devon
817 Tim Curtis v. Notts and Hampshire
818 Notts, by four wickets at Worcester
819 Porth-cawl
820 Collis King v. Notts, 1985
821 John Inchmore, 5-25 v. Oxfordshire, 1986
822 Damian D'Oliveira v. Oxfordshire, 1986
823 Graeme Hick 105 v. Notts at Trent Bridge

JOHN PLAYER LEAGUE - 3

824 Tony Buss (Sussex) at Hastings, 1975
825 Norman Gifford was a victim in all three
826 1975
827 G.M. Turner, 147 v. Sussex at Horsham, 1980
828 W. Larkins (Northants), 158 at Luton, 1982
829 R.A. Hutton (Yorkshire), 7-15 at Leeds, 1969
830 He became the first player to appear for three different Counties in the Sunday League
831 Warwickshire
832 D.R. Turner (Hampshire), 547 av. 34.18
833 B.L. D'Oliveira, 49

PHIL NEALE

834 1975
835 The West Indians
836 At Newark, with 112 v. Notts, 1977
837 Phil Sharpe (Derbyshire), a current Test Selector, caught by Gordon Wilcock at Worcester in 1976
838 Ted Hemsley (first innings) and Glenn Turner (second innings)
839 Lancashire, at Old Trafford, 1975

840 Graham Taylor, currently with Aston Villa
841 England 'B' v. Pakistan, at Leicester in 1982
842 102 v. Northants, at Luton in 1982
843 Norman Gifford
844 Kevin Saxelby at Trent Bridge
845 Leeds
846 Lincolnshire
847 1982
848 Two – 1985 and 1988

1987 REFUGE ASSURANCE LEAGUE

849 Lancashire
850 Stuart Lampitt
851 Gloucestershire
852 Kevin Saxelby
853 Four
854 Swansea
855 Collis King
856 Tim Curtis (617)
857 Neal Radford (25)
858 D.J. Humphries (22)
859 It was the only ball he bowled in the match
860 Paul Pridgeon (8-1-14-2)
861 Four
862 Gordon Lord
863 Derek Aslett (Kent)

GRAEME HICK

864 At The Oval, against Surrey
865 Philip Neale
866 The Young West Indians
867 Kidderminster
868 Moseley
869 Eight

870 174* v. Somerset at Worcester, 1985
871 The Nawab of Pataudi, 1933
872 Eddie Cooper (22 years 265 days), with 216* in 1938
873 Andy Hayhurst (Lancashire) at Worcester
874 Roger Harper (West Indies)
875 Steve Rhodes
876 Denis Compton, aged 70
877 Len Hutton, in 1937
878 Northern Districts

1988 – 1

879 Graham Dilley
880 Graeme Fowler
881 Phil Neale
882 Steve O'Shaughnessy, on his Worcestershire debut against his former County Lancashire
883 Ian Botham and Tim Robinson (Notts)
884 Damian D'Oliveira, 54* off 31 balls: the fastest BBC TV fifty of the season
885 John Birch
886 Ian Botham
887 Frank Chester and Billy Taylor v. Essex, 1914
888 Colin Dredge

1988 – 2

889 At Trent Bridge, by six wickets
890 Graham Rose, for seven
891 M.D. Crowe and J.G. Wyatt – 102 for Somerset, fourth wicket at Worcester
892 C.D. Matthews (Lancs, Western Australia and Australia)
893 Peter Roebuck, regarding his caught and bowled dismissal by Ian Botham
894 Old Hill
895 Swindon

896 Derek Randall (69), Notts winning by one wicket
897 Peter Hartley (Yorkshire)
898 Ian Botham, 5-41 v. Yorkshire at Worcester

PICTURE QUIZ – 9

899 It was shared by R.E.S. Wyatt (centre, seated) and A.F.T.
    White (second from left, seated)
900 Geoff Darks
901 Syd Buller
902 Roy Booth, 65 (Rhodes 3, Buller 1)
903 Rodney Cass
904 Henry (pictured) and Joe Horton
905 Richard Stevens
906 Glamorgan
907 His last first-class appearance at New Road v. Lancashire, in
    1967
908 Brian Statham, caught by Ormrod
909 Bob Carter
910 Kevin Griffith

1988 – 3

911 David Leatherdale
912 Mike Garnham
913 Robin Smith (Hampshire), for his 87*
914 Martin Weston – 50
915 Phil Neale, 132 av. 33.00
916 Hampshire beating Derbyshire
917 Steve Jefferies
918 Yorkshire
919 Tim Curtis
920 Martin Weston

1988 – 4

921 Curtley Ambrose (West Indies)
922 Louis Vorster
923 4-36 in each case v. Leicestershire and Essex
924 Warwickshire at Worcester
925 Peter Roebuck at Worcester
926 Tim Curtis, one of them the Botham wicket
927 Roland Butcher
928 Tim Curtis
929 Hampshire
930 Robin Smith and David Turner bowled eight balls in Worcestershire innings of 17-0 in their ten-wicket win

1988 – 5

931 Yorkshire
932 Martin Weston (72)
933 97
934 By a strange coincidence, Derbyshire at Worcester, in 1984
935 0898 121455
936 Frank Watson, former Old Hill opening batsman and the 'Voice of Worcestershire'
937 M.G. Scothern, who appeared once for the County in 1985
938 Phil Neale with a career best of 98
939 Gloucestershire
940 Tim Curtis caught by Zahid Sadiq off Ian Greig

1988 – 6

941 Richard Illingworth (58) in a ninth-wicket partnership of 113
942 Chris Scott and Kevin Cooper
943 Phil Newport, who had a Worcestershire career best of 77*

944 Richard Ellison (8-112)

945 Steve Coverdale

946 Four

947 The England Selectors, because Graham had withdrawn from the England side through injury

948 Martin Weston

949 Nine dismissals (all catches) in a match to equal the Worcestershire record set by Hugo Yarnold (5 catches, 5 stumpings) in 1949

950 Lancashire

WORCESTERSHIRE ELEVENS

951 H.K. Foster (capt), G.E. Bromley-Martin, E.G. Arnold, R.E. Foster, W.L. Foster, G.F. Wheldon, E.G. Bromley-Martin, A. Bird, R.D. Burrows, G.A. Wilson and T. Straw (wk)

952 W.H. Taylor (capt), F.L. Bowley, F.A. Pearson, G.N. Foster, F. Chester, M.K. Foster, A.F. Lane, A.T. Cliff, R.D. Burrows, J. Harber and E.W. Bale (wk)

953 C.J. Lyttleton (capt), R. Howorth, E. Cooper, B.P. King, C.H. Palmer, H.H.I. Gibbons, S.H. Martin, A.P. Singleton, R.O. Jenkins, J.S. Buller (wk) and R.T.D. Perks

954 A.P. Singleton (capt), R. Howorth, A.F.T. White, E. Cooper, H.H.I. Gibbons, R.E. Bird, D.M. Young, R.O. Jenkins, R.T.D. Perks, J.S. Buller and P.F. Jackson

955 D. Kenyon (capt), M.J. Horton, R.G.A. Headley, T.W. Graveney, D.W. Richardson, R.G. Broadbent, R. Booth (wk), D.N.F. Slade, N. Gifford, J.A. Flavell and R.G.M. Carter

956 D. Kenyon (capt), J.A. Ormrod, R.G.A. Headley, T.W. Graveney, D.W. Richardson, B.L. D'Oliveira, R. Booth (wk), D.N.F. Slade, N. Gifford, J.A. Flavell and L.J. Coldwell

957 N. Gifford (capt), R.G.A. Headley, G.M. Turner, E.J.O. Hemsley, G.R. Cass (wk), J.A. Ormrod, B.L. D'Oliveira, T.J. Yardley, I.N. Johnson, B.M. Brain and J. Cumbes

958 N. Gifford (capt), R.G.A. Headley, G.M. Turner, J.M. Parker, H.G. Wilcock (wk), J.A. Ormrod, B.L. D'Oliveira, T.J. Yardley, J.D. Inchmore, B.M. Brain and V.A. Holder

959 N. Gifford (capt), J.A. Ormrod, G.M. Turner, P.A. Neale, Imran Khan, E.J.O. Hemsley, B.L. D'Oliveira, C.N. Boyns, H.G. Wilcock (wk), J.D. Inchmore and A.P. Pridgeon

960 P.A. Neale (capt), T.S. Curtis, S.J. O'Shaughnessy, G.A. Hick, D.A. Leatherdale, M.J.Weston, S.J. Rhodes (wk), P.J. Newport, N.V. Radford, R.K. Illingworth and A.P. Pridgeon

1988 – 7

961 Graham, whilst his brother was captaining England at Headingley

962 Wayne Noon for Northants, the 1,001st player to appear in the Sunday League

963 Paul Parker

964 David Leatherdale

965 Phil Newport and Ricardo Ellcock

966 Martin Crowe – 132 for Somerset at Worcester

967 Brian Statham (Lancs and England)

968 Tim Munton, 6-21

969 Piran Holloway for Warwickshire

970 Geoff Boycott

1988 – 8

971 1982

972 Greg Thomas (100*), for Glamorgan

973 Steve O'Shaughnessy

974 He became the first batsman to aggregate 2,000 runs for the season

975 73-1 off just 9.3 overs

976 John Derrick

977 Epsom-born Jonathan Robinson
978 10-128
979 Phil Newport, 32*
980 Phil Neale

TIES

981 1980
982 Jack Flavell, 1963
983 Winning the John Player League in 1971
984 Ron Headley, 1972
985 Glenn Turner scoring 1,000 runs (for New Zealand on tour) before the end of May in 1973
986 Ted Hemsley, 1982
987 Winning the County Championship in 1974
988 Eastnor v. Norman Gifford XI during his 1974 benefit season
989 1983
990 Vanburn Holder, 1979

1988 – 9

991 14-1-62-0 at Abergavenny, bowling for a declaration
992 David Leatherdale
993 Essex
994 Steve Rhodes
995 Dermot Reeve
996 Paul Pridgeon
997 David Acfield
998 Neal Radford v. Middlesex
999 Paul Downton
1000 The Cricket Writers Club Young Cricketer of the Year Award to Matthew Maynard

1001 Martin Weston dismissing David Thorne
1002 Surrey
1003 Mike Watkinson (Lancashire)
1004 Peter Walker (Glamorgan and England)
1005 The last wicket, just failing to carry his bat
1006 Tim Curtis returning after retiring hurt
1007 Richard Illingworth with 10-132
1008 Barry Dudleston and Barrie Leadbeater
1009 Geoff Holmes
1010 Five minutes past four o'clock on Friday, 16 September